Risen with Christ: Easter

Also by Hugh Wybrew and published by SPCK:

Orthodox Lent, Holy Week and Easter: Liturgical Texts with Commentary
Orthodox Feasts of Christ and Mary: Liturgical Texts with Commentary

RISEN WITH CHRIST: EASTERTIDE IN THE ORTHODOX CHURCH

Hugh Wybrew

First published in Great Britain 2001
Society for Promoting Christian Knowledge
Holy Trinity Church
Marylebone Road
London NW1 4DU

Biblical quotations are taken from *The New Revised Standard
Version of the Bible* © 1989, 1995.

British Library Cataloguing-in-Publication Data

A catalogue record for this book is available from
the British Library

ISBN 0–281–05343–X

Typeset by Wilmaset Ltd, Birkenhead, Wirral
Printed in Great Britain by
The Cromwell Press, Trowbridge, Wiltshire

Contents

Dedication

τῇ πέτρᾳ τῇ ἀγαπητῇ

FOREWORD

Three Greek words, each of three syllables, mark the climax of Eastern Christendom's year. In candlelit darkness the Easter troparion begins, to be repeated over and over, building to a heart-pounding wave of sound that bridges mortal and eternal, annihilating the universal fear in every human. Echoing the racing drumbeat of the pulse, whether in a tiny church on an island in the Cyclades or, with Justinian, under Hagia Sophia's dome itself, the cry breaks the night:

θανάτῳ θάνατον πατήσας

'By His death He has trodden death under His feet.' Here is the sublime centre from which all liturgy derives, which all rites reflect and celebrate.

If one compares this with the central truth proclaimed in Western, English liturgy, different facets are emphasized. Equally ringing and sublime is the claim, 'I am the resurrection and the life', but the words and viewpoint are Christ's, not man's. Listeners can accept or reject it. Orthodox liturgy assumes the group is sharing the good news and passing it on.

The two languages, too, differ in their strengths. Every translator knows the fluid music of Greek. This derives from the proportion of its vowels to consonants, which in Latin and English is smaller. The majority of Greek words end with a vowel; 'n' and 's' (with its compounds) are almost the only consonants that end words. These final syllables trip the rhythm along in a way utterly different from the marmoreal quality of Rome's Tridentine Mass, or our own *Book of Common Prayer* with its stress on the open vowel (a technique learned from Virgil). All three liturgies have virtues, but they are different.

This book of Orthodox liturgical texts, together with the earlier two in the series, *Orthodox Lent, Holy Week and Easter* and *Orthodox Feasts of Christ and Mary*, all prepared by Hugh Wybrew with commentary, bring the spiritual cast of mind of Orthodox Christianity within reach of Western readers, and provide pasturage for hungry and enquiring souls who are open to fresh enrichment of their deepest beliefs and meditations.

The Byzantine poets, those self-effacing monks dedicated to adorning and enriching the liturgy, simply called themselves 'melodes'. As Greek evolved from a quantitative to an accented language, so the greatest of these hymn-writers, the prolific Romanus, *poeta vere Christianus* of sixth-century Byzantium, slimmed down (though still discursive and metrically elaborate himself) the over-decoration of such predecessors as Ephraem the Syrian, and showed how fewer words led to greater effect. His hymns are 'sermons in poetic form'. So, too, are Hugh Wybrew's lucid, uncluttered translations from the wealth of Orthodox texts. These are arranged so that the whole celebration of Christ's visit to earth and our response to it can be seen through three cycles – Easter, Christmas, and the festivals of the Blessed Virgin Mary – to their culmination in Pentecost and All Saints Day. To go through this experience with Hugh Wybrew as our guide is to emerge grateful, wiser and humbler as we realize once again that in our Father's house are many rooms, and, if we open this door, the world of Eastern spirituality can lend us its unfading golden light to bring us joy.

Francis Warner
St Catharine's College
Cambridge

Introduction

This book is the third in a trilogy which began with *Orthodox Lent, Holy Week and Easter*. That book was followed by *Feasts of Christ and Mary*. Like its predecessors, this book is intended to provide Western Christians with a selection of Orthodox liturgical texts, this time from the services which celebrate the resurrection and ascension of Jesus Christ, and the consequent sending of the Holy Spirit. It is hoped that these texts will enable readers to gain some impression of the themes of Orthodox Eastertide, and will be of help in their personal meditation on the meaning of Easter, Ascension and Pentecost.

Western readers will notice both similarities and differences in the themes of the Sundays in Eastertide in Christian West and East. (The Eastern form of reference to these Sundays also differs from those in current use in the West: the Orthodox 'Second Sunday after Easter' corresponds to the Western 'Second Sunday of Easter', or 'First Sunday after Easter'.) St Thomas' unbelief forms a principal theme on the second Sunday of Easter in both traditions, and the Ascension and Descent of the Holy Spirit are integral to Eastertide in both. Two of the Sundays in Orthodox Eastertide contain themes found in the Western (Roman) lectionary in Lent: the Samaritan Woman, and the Man Born Blind (used in the first of the three cycles of Sunday readings). Both are included in their respective calendars because of their baptismal associations. But whereas the baptismal theme in the West runs through Lent, leading up to Easter, in the East it runs through Eastertide, prolonging one of Easter's central themes. Other Sundays in Orthodox Eastertide have themes not found in the Western calendar in either Lent or Eastertide. They include the commemoration of the first Ecumenical

1

Council of Nicaea in 325. The Ecumenical Councils all took place in the East, and came to be far more prominent liturgically and iconographically in the East than in the West. The visit to the tomb of the Women Bringing Spices and the Healing of the Paralysed Man are peculiar to Orthodox Eastertide, and so is the celebration of Mid-Pentecost. While Western Christians are familiar with the Sunday after Pentecost as Trinity Sunday, in the East that day is the celebration of All Saints.

In the Orthodox Church the services for Eastertide, from the Easter Vigil to the Sunday after Pentecost, the Sunday of All Saints, are contained in the Pentecostarion. This book presents a small selection of texts from the Pentecostarion, used on the principal days of this season: the weekdays of Easter Week, or the Week of Renewal; the Sundays of Eastertide and All Saints' Sunday; and the Feast of Mid-Pentecost. Texts used at the Easter Midnight service are not given here, since they are included in *Orthodox Lent, Holy Week and Easter*. Those who wished to delve deeper into the treasures of Orthodox hymnography during Lent, and at the great festivals of Christ and his Mother, could make use of *The Lenten Triodion* and *The Festal Menaion*, translated by Mother Mary and Bishop Kallistos Ware, and published by Faber. There is unfortunately no companion volume covering Eastertide to which further reference can be made.

Since this book has been written for the general reader, and not for the liturgical specialist, still less for liturgical use, no indication has been given of the particular place occupied by the various texts in the services, beyond indicating which service they come from. The generic name given to the short poetic compositions which form so important a part of Orthodox worship, especially at Vespers and Matins, is *troparion*. In origin they were not unlike the Western antiphon, a short verse attached to a psalm or canticle as a refrain, which reflected the theme of the festival or day. In time in the East they developed an exuberant life of their own, often squeezing out most or all of the psalm or canticle which they had originally enhanced. The many troparia which make up the specific content of the services for each day acquired different names, derived from their function in the service. Using those names would have required a glossary for their explanation, thought an unnecessary complication in such a book.

As in the previous two books, the texts have been freshly translated from the Greek into modern English. Once again I am indebted to Francis Warner, Lord White Fellow and Tutor in English Literature at St Peter's College, Oxford, now Emeritus, for checking and improving my translations, and encouraging me in undertaking the work. For scriptural phrases or allusions I have made use of the New Revised Standard Version of the Bible.

I hope that this book, with the previous two volumes, will help to spread and deepen knowledge of the Orthodox liturgical tradition among Western Christians. They may then make a small contribution to the work of reconciliation between Christians of East and West.

1 THE DEVELOPMENT OF EASTERTIDE IN THE ORTHODOX CHURCH

The life-giving death of Jesus Christ is at the heart of Christian believing and Christian living. It took place at the Jewish feast of Passover, in Greek *Pascha*. Christians celebrated their own Paschal feast, which was originally a unitive festival, commemorating on one day both Christ's death and his resurrection. By the end of the fourth century the Christian Passover had spread over a whole week. It began with Christ's entry into Jerusalem on Palm Sunday, and in some places with the resurrection of Lazarus the day before. It culminated in the celebration of his resurrection at the Easter Vigil. That week came to be preceded by a period of fasting, which eventually extended over the forty days of Lent.

From an earlier time, the Christian Passover was followed by a period of rejoicing in the resurrection of Jesus. Lasting in many churches for fifty days, it was brought to a triumphant conclusion by the celebration of the fiftieth day, Pentecost. In the early centuries, Pentecost often referred, not so much to the final day, but to the whole fifty days of paschal joy.

Jewish Origins

Just as Easter, the Christian Passover, has its origin in the Jewish Passover, so Pentecost, both as a period and a day, derives from Jewish observance. Passover was an ancient pastoral festival, at which an annual sacrifice was offered from the flock. It was celebrated by nomadic Hebrew shepherds before they settled in the land of Canaan, later known as Palestine. In time it came to be linked with Unleavened Bread, an agricultural festival celebrated at the beginning of barley harvest. This was a Canaanite festival, adopted by the

Israelites once they had settled in the land. In New Testament times, the combined festival, lasting for eight days, was often called Passover.

Fifty days after Passover, the Feast of Weeks, another agricultural festival of Canaanite origin, celebrated the end of the wheat harvest. In the Greek translation of the Old Testament, the Septuagint, this feast was called Pentecost, since it took place fifty days after Passover. In the course of Jewish history, these two great pilgrim festivals (like the third, the autumn Feast of Tabernacles), on which all Jews were expected to go up to Jerusalem, came to be celebrated on fixed dates: Passover on the fourteenth day of the month Nisan, and Pentecost fifty days later. These agricultural festivals came to be associated with significant events in the religious history of Israel. From at least the seventh century BC, Passover and Unleavened Bread together commemorated the Exodus from Egypt. In the centuries immediately before Christ, Pentecost was associated with the renewal of the covenant made by God with Noah. By the end of the first century AD, it was observed by at least some Jewish groups as a celebration of the giving of the Law on Mount Sinai.

This association of Pentecost with the giving of the Law was very possibly in Paul's mind when, in his Second Letter to the Corinthians, he contrasts the Law of the old covenant with the Spirit of the new. 'You are a letter of Christ [...] written not with ink but with the Spirit of the living God, not on tablets of stone but on tablets of human hearts [...] our competence is from God, who has made us competent to be ministers of a new covenant, not of letter but of spirit; for the letter kills, but the Spirit gives life' (2 Corinthians 3.3–6). The link was certainly firmly made in later Christian thought.

The New Testament

In his Gospel and in the Acts of the Apostles, Luke reflects the pattern of the Jewish calendar. Jesus was crucified at

Passover, and raised on the third day. During forty days the risen Christ appeared to the apostles, speaking to them of the kingdom of God. Then, on the Mount of Olives, he was taken from them, and a cloud took him out of their sight. The appearances of the risen Jesus came to an end. Ten days later, on the day of Pentecost, the Holy Spirit came to them when they were all together in one place. The pattern of the fifty days in Luke's writings became in time that of Eastertide in the Christian calendar.

It is not however universal in the New Testament. The earliest Gospel, that according to Mark, originally ended with the empty tomb, and made no mention of either the ascension of Christ or the coming of the Holy Spirit. The present ending is a later addition. Matthew ended his Gospel with the manifestation on a mountain in Galilee of the risen Christ, who promises to be with his disciples to the end of the age. Again, there is no reference to either Christ's ascension or the coming of the Spirit. In John's Gospel, the risen Christ bestows the Holy Spirit on the disciples on the evening of Easter Day. By implication his ascension takes place between his appearance to Mary Magdalen that same day, and the following Sunday, when he appears to the disciples and Thomas. Mary is forbidden to touch Jesus, because he has not yet ascended to the Father; Thomas is invited to put his finger into Christ's wounded side. Just as for John Jesus' death and resurrection are inseparable, and his death is the moment of his glorification, so resurrection, ascension and the coming of the Holy Spirit are seen as aspects of one indivisible reality. All three were in fact held together in the early Christian observance of the fifty days of Eastertide, and only separated into distinct commemorations later.

The Early Christian Pentecost

From earliest times Christians celebrated Easter, the Christian Passover, with fifty days of rejoicing. There were differences of calculation, related to differences in Jewish calendrical observance. The practice of the Sadducees was to keep Pentecost on the day after the Sabbath, on Sunday. The Pharisees calculated Pentecost from the 15th Nisan, whichever day of the week it might be. Most parts of the church always celebrated Easter on a Sunday, and kept Pentecost, the fiftieth day, also on a Sunday. But others, notably in Asia Minor, kept Easter on the 14/15th of the Jewish month Nisan, and so celebrated Pentecost fifty days later, on whichever day it fell. In time the former practice prevailed. The practice of keeping Easter, and so Pentecost, on a Sunday was finally established by the Council of Nicaea in 325. But all kept the fifty days as a celebration of the death, resurrection and ascension of Jesus Christ, and the coming of the Holy Spirit. They were a time of continuous rejoicing, in which neither fasting nor kneeling for prayer was allowed. For the season of Pentecost was an anticipation of the resurrection of all in the age to come, and a manifestation of the glory of the kingdom of God.

As such, Pentecost was a most suitable season for baptism. Tertullian, in his treatise on baptism, says that

the Passover provides the day of most solemnity for baptism, for then was accomplished our Lord's passion into which we are baptised [. . .] After that, Pentecost is a most joyful period for arranging baptisms, in which also the resurrection of the Lord was frequently made known to the disciples, and the grace of the Holy Spirit first given, and the hope of the coming of the Lord was indirectly revealed, in that then, when he had been received back into the heavens, the angels said to the apostles that he would come in the same manner in which he had ascended into the heavens, certainly at Pentecost.

For Tertullian, the fifty days of Easter were a celebration not only of the resurrection and ascension of Christ and of the gift of the Holy Spirit, but also of the hope of Christ's return.

In time particular attention began to be given to the Day of Pentecost itself. Early in the fourth century, Eusebius of Caesarea speaks of the fiftieth day as the seal of the fifty days of Pentecost, and as the celebration of the ascension of the Saviour into heaven and the descent of the Holy Spirit among humankind. Luke's sequence of events had not yet inspired a distinct celebration of the ascension forty days after Easter. But at the beginning of the fourth century, the Council of Elvira in AD 300 reinforced the importance of the fiftieth day in its own right. Pentecost was coming to denote the fiftieth day, rather than the fifty days, even though the Council of Nicaea in 325, in its canon forbidding kneeling during Pentecost, still uses the word to refer to the period rather than the day. By that time, too, some Christians were beginning to fast again after the fortieth day, on which the bridegroom had been taken away, so shortening the time of paschal rejoicing. They could appeal to the reference to appearances of Christ during forty days after his resurrection in Acts 1.3. It is not clear whether or not at this stage the fortieth day was being observed as a commemoration of the ascension; but the unitive celebration of Pentecost was beginning to disintegrate.

The Consolidation of the Calendar

Towards the end of the fourth century Egeria, a Western pilgrim to the Holy Land, describes how the church in Jerusalem observed the Easter season. She speaks of the eight days of Easter, showing that the octave was given special importance, perhaps in imitation of the eight days of the Jewish feast of Passover and Unleavened Bread. It was during this octave that the newly baptized were instructed in the meaning of the rites of initiation, through which they had passed on Easter night. By the fourth century, if not earlier, Easter had become the time when baptism was celebrated with special solemnity during the Easter Vigil. Those who

9

were baptized, chrismated (the Eastern equivalent of the Western confirmation) and participated for the first time in the Eucharist were united with Christ in his death and resurrection. They received the gift of the Holy Spirit, the herald and foretaste of the kingdom of God, that heavenly banquet of which the eucharistic meal was the sign and sacrament. In Jerusalem, as elsewhere, there was no fasting throughout the fifty days, and the usual services were held.

On the fiftieth day the usual morning service took place in the Martyrium, the great church built close to the site of the crucifixion. But it was shortened, to enable the bishop, clergy and people to go to the church on Mount Sion. There, on the traditional site of the event, the coming of the Holy Spirit was celebrated: the readings were Acts 2.1–21 and John 14.15–24. Later in the day there was another service on the Mount of Olives, at the site called Imbomon. There the ascension of Christ was commemorated, with appropriate scripture readings and hymns.

Egeria speaks of the fortieth day after the resurrection as a special observance, and this has sometimes been understood to be a celebration of the ascension. But the service itself was held at Bethlehem, and was in all probability a commemoration of the Holy Innocents. By the end of the fourth century, however, in the regions of Antioch and Constantinople, the ascension was being celebrated on the fortieth day. Where this was the case, the Day of Pentecost became a celebration only of the descent of the Holy Spirit. A distinct feast of the ascension entered the calendar of the church of Jerusalem in the first half of the fifth century, although there was still an observance on Pentecost Sunday at the traditional place of the ascension on the Mount of Olives. It is possible, too, that there was already a festival of Mid-Pentecost by the fourth century. Early in the fifth century Peter Chrysologus claimed the authority of the apostolic fathers for such an observance; and the Council of Nicaea in 325 ordered synods of bishops to be held before the fortieth day of the paschal season.

In time both the Ascension and Pentecost acquired their own octaves, and like Easter came to be celebrated for eight days. Eastertide came to an end on the eve of the Ascension, whose octave then occupied most of the remaining days until the Day of Pentecost. The clear pattern of the early Christian Pentecost, fifty days of rejoicing in the eternal kingdom of God, inaugurated by the resurrection of Jesus, became obscured. Resurrection, ascension and the coming of the Holy Spirit, which both John's Gospel and the early Christian tradition had held inseparably together, now became distinct celebrations. The Wednesday and Friday fast was resumed after Easter Week itself, departing from ancient tradition and the rule of the Council of Nicaea, and still further obscuring the original significance of the fifty days of Pentecost as a period. The coming of Christ disappeared altogether as a theme of Eastertide.

The developments which took place in and after the fourth century set the pattern for Eastertide in the Orthodox Church in the Byzantine Empire. Easter remained a time when baptism was celebrated in Constantinople as part of the Easter Vigil at least up to the tenth century. In the lectionary, a sequence of gospel readings for the Sundays of Eastertide evolved, which continued the baptismal theme up to the Ascension. In place by the tenth century, they have given their names to the five Sundays following Easter Day. Although in time Christian initiation ceased to be a normal part of the Easter Vigil in the Orthodox Church, traces of its former presence have remained in the Easter liturgy. Instead of the Trisagion on Easter Day is sung this verse from St Paul's Letter to the Galatians: 'As many of you as were baptized into Christ have clothed yourselves with Christ.' It is sung daily in Easter Week, and again on the Day of Pentecost, where it serves as a reminder of the ancient unitive celebration of Eastertide. By the tenth century, too, the seventh Sunday had come to be a commemoration of the first six ecumenical councils. Subsequently, its commemoration was confined to the first Council of Nicaea in 325. The celebration of all the saints on the Sunday after Pentecost was also in place by the tenth century.

The Pattern of Orthodox Eastertide

This then is the pattern of Eastertide in the Orthodox Church in its fully developed form:

– The resurrection of Jesus Christ is celebrated on *Easter Day*, or *Pascha*. Matins of Easter Day begins at midnight on Holy Saturday, and is followed by the Liturgy.
– The week after Easter Day is called *The Week of Renewal*, or *Bright Week*. Friday is kept as a celebration of the Mother of God as fountain of salvation.
– The second Sunday after Easter – the first day of the second week after Easter – is the last day of the Easter octave, called in Greek *Antipascha*. It is also *The Sunday of Thomas*.
– The third Sunday after Easter is *The Sunday of the Women bringing Spices*.
– The fourth Sunday after Easter is *The Sunday of the Paralysed Man*.
– Wednesday in the fourth week of Easter is the *Feast of Mid-Pentecost*.
– The fifth Sunday after Easter is *The Sunday of the Samaritan Woman*.
– The sixth Sunday after Easter is *The Sunday of the Man Born Blind*.
– Wednesday in the sixth week brings the celebration of *Easter* to a close.
– Thursday in the sixth week is *The Ascension of the Lord*. The celebration of the Ascension lasts for eight days.
– The seventh Sunday after Easter is *The Sunday of the 318 Holy Fathers of the Holy First Council of Nicaea*. In the tenth century this was a celebration of the first six ecumenical councils.

– Friday in the seventh week brings the celebration of the Ascension to a close.

– Saturday in the seventh week is a *Commemoration of all the Departed*.

– The eighth Sunday after Easter is *The Sunday of Pentecost*. The octave concludes on the Saturday after Pentecost.

– The Sunday after Pentecost is *The Sunday of All the Saints*. It is not within the fifty days, but is theologically closely related with Pentecost.

The development of Eastertide in the early centuries led to an essentially similar pattern in the Western Christian calendar. Easter, Ascension and Pentecost had their own octaves, and were celebrated for eight days. The Paschal, or Easter, candle, which was lit at the Easter Vigil, and burned at all subsequent services, was extinguished after the gospel on Ascension Day. Mid-Pentecost was not celebrated in the West, nor was there a special commemoration of the departed. In the West that came to be fixed on 2 November. The Sunday after Pentecost came, in the Middle Ages, to be celebrated as a distinct Feast of the Holy Trinity, and All Saints Day came to be celebrated on 1 November. The earlier unitive observance of the fifty days of Pentecost was no less obscured in the West than in the East.

Its recovery in the Roman Catholic Church was one of the fruits of the liturgical reforms inspired by the Second Vatican Council. Easter retained its octave, although those of Ascension and Pentecost were abolished. The Easter candle is lit throughout the fifty days, which come to an end on Pentecost Sunday. 'Ordinary Time' begins on the Monday after Pentecost. The Anglican and other Western churches have also generally returned to the early Christian observance of the fifty days as an extended celebration of the resurrection and entry into glory of the risen Christ, and the sending of the Holy Spirit.

2 EASTER WEEK

Easter Week is known as Bright Week, or the Week of Renewal. Its services are always fully sung, and are shorter than usual. Vespers and Matins begin in a special way. The officiant stands in front of the altar, holding a censer in his right hand, and a cross and lighted candle in his left. He opens the veil drawn across the entrance to the sanctuary, and begins the office with the opening blessing used at the beginning of the Easter night service:

> Glory to the holy, life-giving and undivided Trinity, one in being, always, now and ever, and to the ages of ages.

Then the Easter troparion is sung three times:

> Christ has risen from the dead,
> by death defeating Death,
> and those buried in the grave
> he has brought back to life.

Matins throughout the week is almost the same as on Easter Night, and the Easter Canon, composed by St John of Damascus in the eighth century, is sung in full daily. Throughout the week the services proclaim and praise the resurrection of Jesus Christ, and each day hymns in praise of the resurrection from the Sunday services in the 'Book of Eight Tones' (*Ochtoechos*) are sung during Lauds. The Royal Doors in the icon screen are left open during Easter Week, symbolizing the gates of Paradise, opened for us by the death and resurrection of Christ. On Friday of Easter Week the Blessed Virgin Mary is celebrated as the fountain of salvation.

The icon of Easter depicts the descent of Christ into hell after his crucifixion. Triumphant and glorious, he holds in his hand the cross, the trophy of victory, and stands on the broken gates of Hades. Beneath his feet the figure of Death cowers defeated. The risen Christ takes by the hand Adam, and often Eve as well, drawing them out of their graves. Behind them David and Solomon, and other figures of the Old Covenant, wait their turn to be raised to life.

The icon of the Life-giving Fountain depicts a fountain, and in its bowl the Mother of God with the Christ-child, blessing with his right hand. He may hold the book of the Gospels, with the incription, 'I am the living water'. Angels may hold a crown over Mary's head with one hand, holding in the other scrolls, proclaiming her as the spotless, divine and life-giving fountain. From the fountain flow streams of water into a pool below. People wash in the water, and drink from it, and so share in the healing and salvation which flow from Christ, born of Mary.

Easter Monday

FROM VESPERS

Come let us worship him
who was begotten of the Father
before time began,
God the Word, incarnate
of the Virgin Mary.
For he endured the cross
and gave himself to the tomb,
as he himself willed;
and rising from the dead
he has saved me,
human being gone astray.

Erasing the record
that stood against us,
Christ our Saviour
has nailed it to the cross

and destroyed the power of Death.
Let us worship his rising
on the third day.

With archangels let us praise
Christ's resurrection.
For he is our redeemer
and the saviour of our souls;
and in fearful glory
and with mighty power
he will come again
to judge the world he formed.

The angel proclaimed you Lord,
you, crucified and buried;
and he said to the women:
Come, see where he lay.
For he has risen, as he said,
like one all-powerful.
So we worship you,
alone immortal.
Christ, Giver of life,
have mercy on us.

By your cross you destroyed
the curse of the tree,
by your burial you slew
the power of Death,
by your rising you enlightened
the race of humankind.
So we cry out to you:
Glory to you,
Christ our benefactor
and our God!

To you, Lord, in fear
the gates of Death were opened

and hell's warders were afraid
when they saw you.
For you shattered
the doors of bronze
and cut in two
the bars of iron;
and you brought us
out of darkness
and the shadow of death
and broke our bonds asunder.

Raising the hymn of salvation,
let us open our mouths in song.
Come, let us all bow down
in the Lord's house and say,
You were crucified on the tree,
and rose from the dead,
and are in the Father's bosom:
make atonement for our sins.

The shadow of the Law has passed away,
now that grace has come.
For as the bush blazed
but was not consumed,
so has the Virgin given birth,
yet remained a virgin.
Instead of the pillar of fire
has the sun of righteousness arisen;
instead of Moses has come Christ,
our souls' salvation.

FROM MATINS
From the Easter Canon

Come, let us drink
a new draught,

not drawn by miracle
from barren rock,
but from immortality's source,
welling from the tomb of Christ,
in whom we stand firm.

Now are all things
filled with light,
heaven and earth
and under the earth.
So all creation celebrates
Christ's resurrection,
on which it stands secure.

Yesterday was I buried
with you, O Christ,
today am I raised
with your risen self.
I was crucified
with you yesterday:
glorify me, Saviour,
in your kingdom.

Coming before dawn
the women with Mary
found the stone
rolled away from the tomb
and heard from the angel:
Why look among the dead,
as though for a human,
for him who dwells
in eternal light?
See the burial cloths.
Run and tell the world
the Lord has risen,
by death defeating Death.

For he is God's Son,
who saves the human race.

FROM LAUDS

Everything that breathes
and every creature
praises you, O Lord;
for by the cross
you have destroyed Death,
that you might show the peoples
your resurrection from the dead,
you who alone love humankind.

Rejoice, you peoples,
and be joyful.
The angel sat
on the stone of the tomb.
He told us the good news:
Christ has risen from the dead,
the Saviour of the world,
and has filled all things
with a sweet fragrance.
Rejoice, you peoples,
and be joyful.

Easter Tuesday

FROM VESPERS

By your cross,
Christ our Saviour,
you broke the power of Death
and destroyed the devil's deceit.
The human race,
saved by faith,
ever sings your praise.

You enlightened all things
by your resurrection, Lord,
and opened Paradise again.
All creation lauding you
ever sings your praise.

I glorify the power
of the Father and of the Son,
and praise the might
of the Holy Spirit,
undivided, uncreated Godhead,
Trinity one in being,
reigning for ever.

Your precious cross,
O Christ, we venerate,
and we praise and glorify
your resurrection.
For by your wounds
we all are healed.

We praise the Saviour
incarnate of the Virgin.
For he was crucified for us,
and rose again the third day,
bestowing on us great mercy.

Descending to those in hell
Christ proclaimed good news.
Take heart, he said,
I have conquered.
I am the resurrection,
I will raise you up,
destroying the gates of hell.

We who stand unworthy
in your holy house

raise our evening hymn,
Christ our God, crying out
from the depths of our hearts:
You have enlightened the world
by your resurrection on the third day:
rescue your people
from the hand of your enemy,
for you love humankind.

FROM MATINS
From the Easter Canon

Keeping divine watch,
may Habbakuk,
who speaks of God,
stand with us,
and show the angel
who brings light,
and thrillingly says:
Today is the world's salvation,
for Christ has risen
as one almighty.

As male Christ appeared,
opening the Virgin's womb.
As mortal he was called Lamb.
Spotless is our Passover,
as one without stain;
and as true God
is he proclaimed.

As a year-old lamb
Christ our blessed crown
sacrificed himself
willingly for all,
a purifying Passover.

Again from the tomb
in beauty has he shone on us,
the Sun of righteousness.

God's ancestor David
danced and leapt
before the shadow ark.
God's holy people, we
see symbols' fulfilment;
let us rejoice
with God-given joy,
for Christ has risen
as one almighty.

FROM LAUDS

Come, all you peoples,
know the power
of the fearful mystery.
For Christ our Saviour,
the Word in the beginning,
has been crucified for us,
and has willed to be buried,
and has risen from the dead,
to save all things.
Him we venerate.

With joy are all things filled,
having proof of the resurrection.
For Mary Magdalen came to the tomb.
She found an angel
in dazzling clothes
sitting on the stone.
He said, Why do you look
for the living among the dead?
He is not here, but has risen,

as he said, going ahead of you
to Galilee.

In your light, Master,
shall we see light,
for you love humankind.
You have risen from the dead,
giving salvation to the human race,
that all creation might praise you,
who alone are without sin.
Have mercy on us.

Easter Wednesday

FROM VESPERS

We venerate without ceasing,
Christ our God, your life-giving cross,
and glorify your resurrection on the third day.
For by it, almighty one,
you have renewed corrupt human nature,
and shown us the way back to heaven,
for you alone are good and love humankind.

You have released us, Saviour,
from the punishment
of the tree of disobedience,
when you willed to be nailed
to the tree of the cross.
You went down to hell, mighty one,
and as God you broke
the bonds of Death.
So we venerate
your resurrection from the dead,
and cry out in joy:
Almighty Lord, glory to you!

You broke down the gates of hell,
Lord, and by your death
you destroyed Death's dominion.
You freed the human race
from corruption,
and gave to the world
life and immortality
and great mercy.

Come, all peoples,
let us praise the Saviour's
resurrection on the third day,
by which we have been released
from the unloosed bonds of hell,
and have received life and immortality,
crying out: You have been crucified
and buried and have risen:
save us by your resurrection,
for you alone love humankind.

Angels and humankind, Saviour,
praise your resurrection,
by which are enlightened
the ends of the earth,
and we all are delivered
from the enemy's enslavement.
So we cry out:
Almighty, life-giving Saviour,
save us by your resurrection,
for you alone love humankind.

The bronze doors you have destroyed
and their bars you have smashed,
Christ our God, and fallen humankind
you have raised up.
So we cry out with one voice:

Lord, you have risen from the dead,
glory to you!

Lord, your begetting of the Father
is timeless and eternal;
your incarnation of the Virgin
is beyond human speech and thought.
Your descent into hell is fearsome
to the devil and his angels;
for having defeated Death
you rose again the third day,
giving immortality to humankind
and great mercy.

FROM MATINS
From the Easter Canon

Let us awake the dawn,
and instead of ointment
let us bring song to the Lord;
and we shall see Christ,
the Sun of righteousness,
the life of all things,
rising from the dead.

Those held fast by bonds of hell
saw your boundless compassion;
with joyful feet they sped
to the light, O Christ,
praising the eternal Passover.

Carrying our lamps
let us go to meet Christ
as he comes from the tomb
like a bridegroom.
With the heavenly hosts

who love to praise,
let us celebrate
God's saving Passover.

FROM LAUDS

By your cross, O Christ,
you have freed us
from the ancient curse.
By your death
you have destroyed the devil,
tyrant over human nature.
By your rising
you have filled all things with joy.
So we acclaim you:
Glory to you, Lord,
risen from the dead!

By your cross, Christ our Saviour,
guide us into your truth,
and deliver us
from the snares of the enemy.
You have risen from the dead:
at the intercession of your saints, Lord,
stretch out your hand and raise us,
who have fallen into sin,
for you love humankind.

You did not leave the Father's bosom,
Only-begotten Word of God,
when you came to earth
in your love for humankind,
and without change became human.
In the body you endured
the cross and death,
though as God you could not suffer.

Having risen from the dead,
you have given immortality
to the human race,
since you alone are almighty.

Easter Thursday

FROM VESPERS

By your revered cross, O Christ,
you have put to shame the devil;
by your resurrection
you have drawn the sting of sin;
you have saved us from Death's jaws.
We give you glory,
Only-begotten Son.

You were led as a sheep to the slaughter,
who gave resurrection to the human race.
At this hell's rulers were terrified,
and the baleful gates were lifted up.
For Christ the King of glory entered;
Come out! he said, to those in chains,
to those in darkness, Show yourselves!

A great wonder! The Creator
of the invisible realms,
for love of humankind
has suffered in the flesh
and, immortal, has risen.
Come, races and peoples,
and give him worship.
For in his compassion
he has saved us from error,
and taught us to praise
one God in three persons.

Our evening worship we offer you,
the Light which never sets.
At the end of the ages,
in the flesh as in a mirror,
you shone on the world.
You went down into hell;
there you scattered the darkness,
and displayed resurrection light
to the peoples.
Glory to you, giver of light!

Let us give glory to Christ,
the pioneer of our salvation.
When he rose from the dead
the world was saved from error.
The host of angels rejoices,
the deceit of demons flees.
Fallen Adam arises,
the devil is crushed.

Lord, you emptied hell
and defeated Death.
Our Saviour,
you enlightened the world
by your precious cross:
have mercy on us.

FROM MATINS
From the Easter Canon

You descended to earth's depths,
and smashed the eternal bars,
which held the captives fast.
On the third day,
like Jonah from the whale,
you rose from the tomb.

When you rose from the tomb,
O Christ, you kept the seals
unbroken. When you were born
you kept the Virgin's key intact.
But for us you opened
the gates of Paradise.

My Saviour, victim
living and unslain,
as God you willingly
offered yourself
to the Father.
Rising from the tomb,
you raised with you
all Adam's race.

FROM LAUDS

Lord, you came out of the tomb,
sealed by lawless men,
as you were born of the Virgin:
your bodiless angels knew not
how you were incarnate.
The soldiers guarding you
felt nothing when you rose.
For both were sealed
to those who tested them.
But the marvels stand revealed
to those who with faith
venerate the mystery.
To us who praise it
give joy and great mercy.

Lord, crushing the eternal bars
and breaking the chains,
you rose from the tomb,

leaving your burial cloths
in witness of the three days
you lay buried in the tomb.
Guarded in the cave,
you went ahead in Galilee.
Great is your mercy,
unconquered Saviour:
have mercy on us.

Lord, the women ran to the tomb
to see you, O Christ,
who had suffered for us.
When they came, they found
an angel sitting on the stone,
rolled away in fear.
He called out to them,
saying: The Lord is risen.
Tell his disciples,
he who saves us
has risen from the dead.

Lord, as you came out,
although the tomb was sealed,
so you came in
to your disciples,
although the doors were shut.
You showed them the wounds
your body had suffered,
which you accepted, Saviour,
in your long sufferance.
As one of David's line
you endured wounds;
as Son of God
you freed the world.
Great is your mercy,

unconquered Saviour,
have mercy on us and save us.

Easter Friday

FROM VESPERS

Winning victory over hell,
you ascended the cross,
O Christ, to raise up with you
those who sat in Death's darkness,
for you are free among the dead.
You pour forth life
from your own proper light:
Almighty Saviour,
Have mercy on us.

Today Christ, defeating Death,
rose as he said,
and gave joy to the world;
that we all, crying out,
may give him this praise:
Fountain of life,
unapproachable light,
Almighty Saviour,
have mercy on us.

Where can we sinners flee
from you, Lord, who are present
in all your creation?
To heaven? There you dwell.
To hell? You have defeated Death.
To the depths of the sea?
There is your hand, Lord.
We seek refuge in you,
before you we fall
prostrate and pray:

You have risen from the dead:
have mercy on us.

In your cross, O Christ,
we make our boast,
and we praise and glorify
your resurrection.
For you are our God,
you alone we acknowledge.

Glory to your might, Lord,
for you have crushed him
who held the power of death.
By your cross you have renewed us,
giving us life and immortality.

Always blessing the Lord,
we praise his resurrection.
For he endured the cross,
by death destroying Death.

FROM MATINS
From the Easter Canon

He who rescued the three young men
from the furnace
became human and suffered
as a mortal;
and through his sufferings
he clothed what is mortal
in the beauty of immortality.
He alone is blessed,
the God of our ancestors,
and highly glorified.

The women, wise in God's ways,
hastened after you with ointment.

They sought you with tears
as a mortal; rejoicing
they worshipped you,
the living God,
and brought to your disciples,
O Christ, the good news
of the mystical Passover.

Death's slaying,
hell's destruction,
new, eternal life's beginning:
these we celebrate.
With exultation we praise
him who caused them all,
the God of our ancestors,
who alone is blessed,
and highly glorified.

Truly holy and celebrated
is this night, redemptive
and bright shining;
heralding the radiant
day of the resurrection,
in which the eternal light
in bodily form from the tomb
shone forth on all.

Pure Mother of God,
who gave birth,
in way beyond telling,
to the Father's eternal Word,
open my mouth, holy Lady,
and lead me to praise you,
that I may exalt you,
crying out to you, the fountain:
Hail, fount of delight ever-welling;

hail, stream of beauty past telling.
Hail, every sickness' destruction;
hail, varied passions' purgation.
Hail, clearest river, curing believers;
hail, water most pleasing to every kind of sufferer.
Hail, stream of wisdom, ignorance dispelling;
hail, heart's mingled wine, ambrosia outpouring.

FROM LAUDS

Your cross, Lord,
is your people's
life and resurrection;
and trusting it
we praise you, our God,
who rose from the dead.
Have mercy on us.

Your burial, Lord,
has opened Paradise
to the human race.
Released from corruption
we praise you, our God,
who rose from the dead.
Have mercy on us.

With Father and Spirit
Christ let us praise,
who rose from the dead,
and cry out to him:
You are our life
and resurrection.
Have mercy on us.

On the third day, O Christ,
you rose from the tomb,
as it is written,

raising with you
our forefather Adam.
So the human race glorifies you
and praises your resurrection.

The water from the fountain
brings salvation
to all who are weak.
Come we near then with faith,
and draw grace for ourselves.

Immortal source's life-giving well
grants to all who draw near with love
an inexhaustible flood of healing.

Water from the Virgin strengthens souls.
We who are defiled by passions,
let us make haste to the Maiden
and cleanse ourselves of them.

Now the holy vessel plenteously
pours forth to those who ask
manna from the ever-flowing source.
Let each draw out according to their need.

Easter Saturday

FROM VESPERS

Our evening praise
and our spiritual worship
we bring you, O Christ,
for you have been pleased
to have mercy on us
by your resurrection.

Lord, Lord, cast us not out
from your presence;

but be pleased
to have mercy on us
by your resurrection.

Rejoice, holy Sion,
mother of the churches
and dwelling of God;
for you were first
to receive remission of sins
by the resurrection.

The Word, who was begotten
of God the Father before all ages,
and in the last times became incarnate
of her who was a virgin,
by his own will suffered
crucifixion and death;
and saved humankind long dead,
by his own resurrection.

Your resurrection from the dead,
O Christ, we praise,
for by it you have set free
the race of Adam from hell's sway,
and as God you have given the world
eternal life, and great mercy.

Glory to you, Saviour Christ,
only-begotten Son of God,
for you were nailed to the cross
and the third day rose from the tomb.

We glorify you, Lord,
who willingly for us
endured the cross,
and we worship you.
Almighty Saviour,
cast us not out

from your presence,
but hear us
and have mercy on us
by your resurrection,
for you love humankind.

The King of heaven,
for love of humankind
appeared on earth
and went about among us.
He took flesh of a pure Virgin,
and came forth from her incarnate.
One Son is he, twofold in nature
but not so in person.
So we proclaim him perfect God
and perfect in humanity,
and confess Christ to be our God.
Mother yet virgin, plead with him
to have mercy on our souls.

You ascended the cross, Jesus,
who descended from heaven.
You, life immortal,
came down to die.
To those in darkness
you came, the true light;
to those who had fallen,
the resurrection of all.
Our light and our Saviour,
glory to you!

FROM MATINS
From the Easter Canon

Shine, shine, new Jerusalem,
for the glory of the Lord

has risen upon you.
Dance for joy now, Sion,
and rejoice. And you,
pure Mother of God,
be joyful at the resurrection
of him to whom you gave birth.

Loving voice divine,
voice most sweet!
For you have promised truly,
O Christ, to be with us
to the end of the age.
Having this hope for anchor,
we who believe rejoice.

O Christ, great and holiest Passover!
O wisdom and Word and power of God!
Grant us more truly to partake of you
in the endless day of your kingdom.

The Easter Canticles

Let God rise up, let his enemies be scattered;
let those who hate him flee before him.

The sacred Passover today
has been revealed to us:
Passover new and holy,
mystical Passover,
Passover most revered,
the Passover which is Christ the Redeemer;
Passover immaculate,
great Passover,
Passover of believers,
the Passover which opens for us
the gates of Paradise,

the Passover which sanctifies
all who believe.

As smoke is driven away, so drive them away;
as wax melts before the fire.

Come from what you have seen,
O women who bring good news,
and say to Sion:
Receive from us
the joyful good news
of Christ's resurrection.
Make merry, dance for joy,
rejoice, Jerusalem,
for you see Christ the King
coming forth from the tomb
as a bridegroom.

Let the wicked perish before God,
but let the righteous be joyful.

The women bringing spices,
very early in the morning,
stood before the tomb
of him who gives life,
and found an angel sitting on the stone.
He spoke to them and said,
Why do you look for the living
among the dead?
Why do you mourn in death
what is immortal?
Go and tell his disciples.

This is the day that the Lord has made;
let us rejoice and be glad in it.

Passover, joyful Passover,
Passover of the Lord!
The most revered Passover
has risen on us.
Passover! With joy
embrace we one another.
Passover, release from grief!
For today, from the tomb,
as from a bridal chamber,
has Christ shone forth;
he has filled the women
with joy and told them:
Proclaim the good news
to the apostles!

Glory to the Father and to the Son and to the Holy Spirit, now and ever and to the ages of ages. Amen.

Day of resurrection!
Let us rejoice in the feast,
and embrace one another.
Let us say, Brothers and sisters!
even to those who hate us;
let us forgive all things
because of the resurrection,
and in these words cry out:
Christ has risen from the dead,
by death defeating Death,
and those buried in the grave
he has brought back to life.

The services of Easter Week are a sustained paean to the Risen Christ. Heaven and earth unite to praise him who by his death has destroyed the power of Death, and by his resurrection has reconciled humankind with God. Sins are forgiven, and with Christ we are raised from the death of sin to the new life of the resurrection. The darkness of error has been dispersed, and we live now in the light of Christ, who has brought us true knowledge of God. For he who was crucified and rose from the dead is the incarnate Word of God, the Second Person of the Trinity, whom we worship with the Father and the Holy Spirit. God the Son became human in the womb of the Virgin; and so she is rightly celebrated as the fountain of healing, life and salvation.

The joyful splendour of Easter Night is prolonged for a full week, not least by the daily use at Matins of the Canon of St John of Damascus, composed in the eighth century. Its hymns, like all the texts sung this week, combine New Testament story with Christian doctrine and Old Testament reference in a superb poetic celebration of the Christian Passover. In that paschal mystery we too can share, through faith in the divine sacrifice offered in Christ's humanity on the cross.

The Easter icon dramatically depicts our participation in Christ's salvation. Its title, 'The Resurrection', is deliberately ambivalent. It shows both the resurrection of Jesus and that of the humanity he died to save, and so enshrines the character of the early Christian paschal festival as a celebration of our salvation. The sign and sacrament of our participation in Christ's new life is baptism. St Paul wrote to the Christians in Rome: 'Do you not know that all of us who have been baptized into Christ Jesus were baptized into his death? Therefore we have been buried with him by baptism into death, so that, just as Christ was raised from the dead by the glory of the Father, so we too might walk in newness of life' (Romans 6.3–4). Throughout Bright Week at the Liturgy the Trisagion is replaced with this verse from St Paul's Letter to the Galatians: 'As many of you as were baptized into Christ have clothed yourself with Christ.' Celebrating Christ's resurrection, we celebrate the first-fruits of our own, and look forward to its fulfilment in the kingdom of God.

3 OCTAVE OF EASTER: SUNDAY OF THOMAS

Second Sunday after Easter

The second Sunday after Easter commemorates the apostle Thomas, who was not present when the risen Christ appeared to the other disciples on the evening of Easter Day. The gospel at the Liturgy is John 20.19–31, which tells of Thomas' refusal to believe in the resurrection unless he can touch the wounds of the crucified Jesus. Only when the living Christ appears again a week later, and invites Thomas to touch his hands and side, does Thomas confess Jesus as his Lord and God. This is the dominant theme of today's liturgical texts. The Canon at Matins, composed by John of Damascus, the author of the Easter Canon, celebrates the resurrection of Christ.

The corresponding icon is that of 'The touch of Thomas'. By contrast with St John's Gospel, where the episode takes place in the house, the risen Christ stands in the open, outside a house. With his left hand he draws aside his garment to display his wounded right side. Thomas is beside him, and with fear stretches out his right hand to touch Christ's side. In the other hand he sometimes holds a scroll on which is written his confession of faith: 'My Lord and my God'. The other apostles look on in awe.

FROM VESPERS

When the doors were shut
and the disciples met together,
you suddenly came in,
all-powerful Jesus, our God.
You stood among them,
gave them peace, and filled them

with the Holy Spirit.
You commanded them to wait
and not leave Jerusalem,
until they were clothed
with power from on high.
And so we cry out to you,
Glory to you, our enlightenment,
resurrection and peace!

Eight days after the resurrection, Lord,
you appeared to the disciples
where they had come together.
Saying to them, Peace be with you,
you showed to the doubting disciple
your hands and purest side.
He believed and cried out to you,
Glory to you,
my Lord and my God!

Thomas, who was called the Twin,
was not with them when you came in,
O Christ, the doors being shut.
Neither did he believe what they told him.
So from doubt you made him firm in faith.
You did not disdain, good Lord,
to show him your side most pure,
and the wounds in your hands and feet.
When he touched and saw,
he confessed you to be
not God alone nor only human,
and cried out,
Glory to you,
my Lord and my God!

When the disciples were uncertain,
on the eighth day the Saviour came

where they were assembled.
Saying, Peace be with you,
he said to Thomas, Come, apostle,
feel the hands in which the nails were fixed.
O happy doubt of Thomas!
He brought believers' hearts to knowledge,
and cried out in fear,
Glory to you,
my Lord and my God!

When the doors were shut, O Christ,
you stood among the disciples.
By divine providence,
Thomas was not then with them.
For he said, I will not believe,
unless I see the Lord myself;
unless I see the side from which
flowed blood, water and baptism;
unless I see the wound from which
humanity's great hurt's been healed;
unless I see he's not a spirit,
but flesh and bones.
Glory to you, Lord,
who defeated death and convinced Thomas.

O wonderful marvel!
John reclined on the breast of the Word;
Thomas was deemed fit to touch his side.
The one drew thence with fear
theology's depths, God's saving plan;
the other was thought fit
to guide us into the mystery.
For he set clearly before us
the proofs of his rising,
crying, Glory to you,
my Lord and my God!

Lover of humankind, great and beyond compare
is the magnitude of your compassion.
For you have patiently endured
the Jews' scourging,
the apostle's touch,
the intrigues of those who denied you.
How could you be incarnate?
How could you be crucified,
you, the one without sin?
But grant us understanding
to cry out like Thomas,
Glory to you,
my Lord and my God!

FROM MATINS

When the disciples were concealed,
for fear of the Jews,
and had gathered on [Mount] Sion,
you came to them, good Lord.
You stood among them,
the doors being locked,
filling them with joy.
You showed them your hands
and your holy side's wounds;
and said to the doubting disciple,
Reach out your hand and see
that it is I myself,
who suffered for you.

Seeing my side
and the marks of the nails,
why, Thomas, do you not believe
in my resurrection? said the Lord,
when he had risen from the tomb,
and had appeared to the disciples

45

in a mysterious way.
The Twin believed,
and cried out to the Creator,
You are my God and my Lord.

Who preserved the disciple's hand
unscorched, when he approached
the fiery side of the Lord?
Who gave him boldness and strengthened
him to touch the flaming bone?
None but the side that was touched:
for if that side had not empowered
the right hand made of clay,
how could it have touched the wounds
which shook the heavens and earth?
This grace was given to Thomas
to touch it, and cry out to Christ,
You are my Lord and God.

You touched with your own hand
the wounds of my limbs:
do not disbelieve me, Thomas,
for I was wounded for you.
Be of one mind with the disciples,
and proclaim the living God.

Spring today is fragrant,
the new creation celebrates.
Today are drawn the bolts
of doors, and of
friend Thomas' doubt,
who cries, My Lord and God!

FROM LAUDS

After your awesome rising,
Giver of Life, from the grave,

as you did not break, O Christ,
the seals of the sepulchre,
so you came in through closed doors
to the apostles, bringing them joy,
and staightway gave them your Spirit,
through your boundless mercy.

Thomas, called also the Twin,
was not present when you appeared,
Lord, to the disciples.
So he doubted your resurrection
and cried to those who saw you,
Unless I put my finger into his side,
and into the mark of the nails,
I will not believe he has risen.

As you wish for touch,
Christ said to Thomas,
Put out your hand and know me,
that I have bones and earthly body.
Do not doubt,
but believe like the others.
He cried out,
You are my Lord and my God;
glory to your resurrection!

Eight days after the resurrection, Jesus,
King and Only-begotten Word of the Father,
you appeared to your disciples,
although the doors were shut,
giving them your peace.
To the doubting disciple
you showed the marks:
Come, touch my hands and my feet,
and my undefiled side.

He believed and cried out to you,
Glory to you, my Lord and my God!

The disciples hastened to the mountain
for his ascension from the earth.
The Lord stood before them,
and they worshipped him.
They learnt of the power
given him everywhere,
and were sent into all the world
to proclaim his resurrection from the dead
and his return into heaven.
You gave your faithful promise
always to be with them,
Christ our God and Saviour.

Thomas is the patron saint of those who find faith in the resurrection of Jesus difficult. One of the troparia exclaims, 'O happy doubt of Thomas!' for it was his refusal to believe what others told him that enabled Jesus to offer tangible proof that he was indeed alive after his death and burial. Yet that evidence of the resurrection is not available to those who live after the return of Jesus to the Father. They include John's first readers; and so in the gospel for the day the evangelist says that he has written in his book this and many other signs done by Jesus, 'so that you may come to believe that Jesus is the Messiah, the Son of God, and that believing you may have life in his name'. We believe in the resurrection of Christ on the authority of the Christian tradition, transmitted to us by the Scriptures in the life of the Christian community. But that faith is confirmed by our own experience of the risen Christ, who comes to us, not only in sacramental worship and personal prayer, but in all our attempts to live as disciples of our risen Lord. To believe in the resurrection of Jesus is to believe in the power of divine love to overcome suffering and death, and so to live hopefully. That is why Christ, when Thomas acknowledges him 'My Lord and my God', says, 'Blessed are those who have not seen and yet have come to believe.'

4 SUNDAY OF THE WOMEN BRINGING SPICES

Third Sunday after Easter

This Sunday is named after the gospel reading, Mark 15.43—16.8, which tells of Jesus' burial by Joseph of Arimathea, and of the three women who came with spices to anoint the dead body, and found the tomb empty. Nicodemus, who in St John's Gospel assists Joseph, is also mentioned in the texts.

Mark speaks of three women, Mary Magdalen, Mary the Mother of James, and Salome. In St Matthew's Gospel there are only two, Mary Magdalen and the other Mary; while St John says that it was Joseph and Nicodemus who brought myrrh and aloes with which to bury Jesus, and that it was Mary Magdalen alone who discovered the tomb empty and met the risen Jesus. Orthodox tradition follows St Luke in holding that it was not only the women named in the other gospels, but also the many women who had followed Jesus from Galilee, who came to anoint and bury him.

Not all today's texts relate to the day's special commemoration. Some celebrate the resurrection itself, while others are in praise of Mary. At Matins three Canons are used, of the Resurrection, of the Mother of God, and of the Women Bringing Spices. This last is attributed to St Andrew of Crete (c.660–740), who composed many hymns, and a number of canons, including the Great Canon used in Lent. The texts relating to the women tell the story of their visit to the tomb, drawing on the various details given in the Gospels, but do so in the light of Christian faith in Jesus Christ as the Second Person of the Trinity, God incarnate.

The icon of the commemoration depicts the Marys standing outside the tomb, modelled on the shrine of the holy sepulchre in Jerusalem. An angel indicates the empty tomb, and tells the good news of the resurrection. This image was perhaps the most popular iconographic allusion to the resurrection until the seventh century. Its first surviving occurrence was found in the early third-century baptistery of the house church at Dura Europos. As an image pointing to the resurrection, the Marys at the tomb gave way, in the course of the seventh century, to the image of the victorious Christ harrowing hell and raising Adam and Eve. But it found a permanent place in the developed iconographic sequence of passion images, following the deposition and entombment, and preceding the resurrection.

FROM VESPERS

The women bringing ointment,
at early dawn taking spices,
came to the Lord's tomb.
Finding what they did not expect,
they pondered cautiously the stone's removal,
and said to one another,
Where are the tomb's seals?
Where is Pilate's guard and the strict security?
But a dazzling angel came to inform
the women, who were at a loss,
and said to them, Why do you with mourning
look for him who is alive,
and brings to life the human race?
Christ our God, who is almighty,
has risen from the dead,
granting us all life and immortality,
enlightenment and great mercy.

Why, O disciples, do you mingle
your spices with tears?
The stone has been rolled way,
the tomb is emptied.
See mortality conquered by life,

the seals bearing clear witness,
the guard set by the disobedient Jews
deeply sleeping.
What is mortal has been saved
by the flesh of God; hell laments.
Hasten with joy and tell his apostles,
Christ has put Death to death,
he is the first-born from the dead,
and he goes ahead of you to Galilee.

The women bringing spices
came to your tomb and saw its seals,
but did not find your undefiled body.
Lamenting they made anxious haste
and said, Who has taken our hope away?
who has taken him, dead, naked and anointed,
his Mother's only consolation?
Oh, how was he slain, who raised the dead?
He who despoiled hell, how was he buried?
But rise from the dead, Saviour,
by your own power on the third day,
as you said, and save us.

Mary Magdalen and the other Mary
came to the tomb, seeking the Lord.
They saw the angel like lightning,
sitting on the stone and saying to them,
Why do you look for the living among the dead?
He has risen, as he said;
you will find him in Galilee.
To him let us cry out,
Glory to you, Lord,
risen from the dead!

Joseph asked for Jesus' body
and put it in his own new tomb.

For it became him to come forth
from the tomb as from a bridal chamber.
You have destroyed the power of Death,
and opened for us the gates of Paradise:
glory to you!

With the help of Nicodemus
Joseph took you down from the tree,
you who wrap yourself in light
as in a garment.
He saw you dead, stripped, unburied,
and in his grief and compassion
he bewailed you:
Ah me, most sweet Jesus!
When the sun just now saw you
hanging on the cross
it wrapped itself in darkness.
The earth shook with fear
and the curtain of the Temple
was torn in two.
Now I see you for my sake
submit to willing death,
How can I bury you, my God?
How can I wrap you in a shroud?
With what hands can I touch your pure body?
What song can I sing at your passing,
O merciful Saviour?
I extol your sufferings,
I praise too your burial
and your resurrection:
O Lord, glory to you!

Noble Joseph took your pure body
down from the tree,
and wrapped it with sweet spices
in a clean linen cloth,

and laid it in a new tomb.
But on the third day
you rose, Lord, and granted
to the world great mercy.

Standing by the tomb
the angel cried
to the women bringing ointment,
Spices are intended for the dead,
while Christ has shown himself
a stranger to corruption.
But proclaim: The Lord has risen,
granting to the world great mercy!

FROM MATINS

The women bringing spices
saw the tomb empty
and said to the apostles,
The strong man has destroyed Death
and released from their bonds
those held captive in hell.
With boldness proclaim,
Christ our God has risen,
giving us great mercy!

When you said to the women
bringing spices, Greetings!
you brought to an end Eve's,
our first mother's, lamenting
by your resurrection, Christ our God;
and you charged them to tell your apostles,
The Saviour has risen from the tomb!

When the women bringing spices
came to your tomb, O Saviour,
they were at a loss and said to one another,

Who will roll away the stone for us
from the tomb? When they looked up,
they saw the stone had been rolled away.
They were astonished at the angel's
appearance and his dress.
They were seized with terror,
and intended to flee.
But the young man said to them,
Do not be afraid: the one you seek
has risen. Come, see the place
where the body of Jesus lay;
and go quickly, tell his disciples,
The Saviour has risen from the tomb!

Praised be the noble counsellor Joseph,
with the women bringing spices
and the divine apostles,
for he too is a herald
of Christ's resurrection.

May we who believe
praise Joseph, worthy of admiration,
and with him Nicodemus
and the faithful women
bringing spices, who cried,
The Lord is risen indeed!

FROM LAUDS

Truly, you who break the law,
when you sealed the tomb
you made us worthy of a greater marvel.
The guards themselves know it.
Today he came out of the tomb;
and they said, Say, while we were asleep
his disciples came and stole him away.

But who steals the dead, especially one naked?
He himself has risen by his own power,
like God, leaving his grave clothes in the tomb.
Come and see, O Jews,
how he has not broken the seals,
he who has defeated Death,
and gives to humankind
unending life and great mercy.

It was very early in the morning
when the women came to your tomb,
O Christ; but the body they sought
was not to be found. Because of this,
since they were at a loss,
those who stood before them
in dazzling clothes said to them,
Why do you look for the living among the dead?
He has risen, as he told you.
Why do you not recall his words?
The women believed them,
and told what they had seen.
But the good news seemed idle words,
so that the disciples still delayed.
But Peter ran and when he saw
he glorified your marvellous deeds.

In Matthew, Mark and Luke the women bringing ointment
and spices are the first witnesses to the resurrection; in John
that role is given to Mary Magdalen alone. They discover the
tomb empty, and are afraid. But the angelic message en-
courages them, and they are sent to tell the male disciples
that Jesus has been raised from death.

Both in the New Testament and in Christian tradition the
women's discovery of the empty tomb witnesses to the truth
of the resurrection. That witness is confirmed, in Matthew's
Gospel, by the almost immediate appearance of the risen

Christ to them, before they can tell the disciples. In Luke it is confirmed by the encounter with Christ of the two disciples on the road to Emmaus; while in John's Gospel Mary Magdalen meets the risen Jesus in the garden, while she is still pondering sadly on his body's disappearance.

The women can be understood as embodying the mission of the Church, the whole Christian community. We cannot experience the empty tomb as they did, although generations of pilgrims to the Church of the Resurrection, or Holy Sepulchre, in Jerusalem have been renewed in faith by the experience of entering the shrine which is on the traditional site of the tomb. But it is possible to encounter the living Christ in the many ways in which he comes to us, in the sacramental life of the Church and in daily encounters with our human sisters and brothers. Those experiences of the risen Christ strengthen our own faith; they are also intended to encourage us to be witnesses, like the women, to God's power to raise human beings from the death of sin to the new and eternal life of his kingdom.

5 Sunday of the Paralysed Man

Fourth Sunday after Easter

This Sunday is named after the gospel passage read at the Liturgy, John 5.1–15. It tells of Jesus healing a man who had been ill for thirty-eight years. Though the gospel does not say so explicitly, tradition presumes the man to have been paralysed, since he could not move by himself. The texts which relate to the paralysed man's cure are derived almost entirely from the passage itself, although occasionally they incorporate details from other miraculous healings. So the troparion 'Jesus went up to Jerusalem' attributes to the paralysed man the medical expenses of the woman suffering from a flow of blood (Mark 5.26); while 'In Solomon's Portico' mistakenly identifies the portico of the Sheep Pool with a portico of the Temple, referred to in connection with the healing of a man born lame (Acts 3.11).

These texts are used together with others celebrating the resurrection, and the Mother of God. At Matins texts from three canons are used, of Easter, of the Mother of God, and of the Paralysed Man. The latter is attributed to Joseph the Hymnographer. Joseph (c.810–886) was the most prolific of Greek hymn-writers. Born in Sicily, he moved to Thessalonica in 830, and about 850 founded a monastery in Constantinople. Sometimes confused with Joseph of Thessalonica, he is said to have composed a thousand canons. In Greek the initial letters of the troparia of the ninth ode of the Canon of the Paralysed Man form the name Joseph.

The icon of the day depicts a pool with five arches beneath it, and in the pool an angel standing. To one side stands Christ, blessing the sick man, and his apostles. The paralysed man, healed, is shown carrying his bed, while other diseased people lie around on their beds.

FROM VESPERS

You came, merciful Christ, who created
humankind by your own pure hand,
to heal the sick; by your own word
you raised the paralytic at the Sheep Pool;
you healed the pain of the woman
who suffered from a haemorrhage;
you had mercy on the Canaanite woman's
daughter, possessed by an unclean spirit;
and the centurion's request you did not ignore.
So we cry out, Glory to you,
Almighty Lord!

Like one dead unburied, the paralysed
man saw you and cried out,
Have mercy on me, Lord,
for my bed has become my grave.
Of what use is life to me?
The Sheep Pool I do not desire:
for I have no one to put me in
when the waters are stirred up.
But to you, the fount of healing,
I come, that I may cry out with all,
Glory to you, Almighty Lord!

Jesus went up to Jerusalem,
to the Sheep Pool called in Hebrew
Bethezda, which has five porticoes.
In these lay many invalids;
for the angel of God came there
at certain seasons, stirring it up,
and gave healing to those
who approached with faith.
And when the Lord saw the man
who had been there a long time
he said to him, Do you want to be made well?

The sick man answered him, Lord,
I have no one to put me into the pool
when the water is stirred up.
On doctors have I spent all that I had,
and have not been deemed fit to find mercy.
But the physician of souls and bodies
said to him, Take your mat and walk,
and proclaim my power and great mercy
to the ends of the earth.

At the Sheep Pool lay a sick man;
and when he saw you, Lord, he called out,
I have no one to put me into it
when the water is stirred up;
while I am making my way,
someone else goes ahead of me
and is healed, while I lie sick.
At once the Lord had compassion and said to him,
For your sake I became human,
for your sake was I clothed with flesh;
and do you say, I have no one?
Take your mat and walk.
All things are possible for you,
Holy One, all things obey you,
all things are subject to you.
Remember us all and have mercy on us,
for you love humankind.

In Solomon's Portico lay many sick people;
and about the middle of the festival
Jesus found a paralysed man who had been
lying there for thirty-eight years.
In a commanding voice he said to him,
Do you want to be made well?
The sick man answered him, Lord,
I have no one to put me into the water

when it is stirred up.
He said to him, Take your bed;
see, you are well, do not sin again.
Through the prayers of the Mother of God,
send down upon us, Lord, great mercy.

FROM MATINS

O Christ, who by your divine word
once strengthened the paralysed man
and commanded him to take up his mat,
though he had long been ailing,
heal my soul, grievously sick.

Once an angel would go down to the Sheep Pool,
and heal one person but once a year.
Now by divine baptism Christ
heals a multitude without number.

Heal my soul, good Lord,
grievously sick for many years,
as you once healed the paralysed man,
that I may walk in your ways,
which you have shown to those who love you.

A single word strengthened the paralysed man,
when the universal Word spoke out,
who for our sake appeared on earth
in his compassion. So he took up his mat
and walked; and the scribes could not endure
seeing what had been done, possessed
by the evil jealousy which paralyses souls.

He who once lay many years in pain,
healed by your command, O Christ,
now gives glory, praising
your compassion, Giver of Life.

As once you raised the paralysed man,
raise up, Lord, with your divine help,
my soul, grievously paralysed
by all kinds of sins and unbecoming deeds;
that healed I may cry out,
Glory, merciful Christ, to your power!

You hold in your hand the ends of the earth,
Christ our God; with the Father you are
without beginning; and with the Holy Spirit
you govern all things. You appeared in flesh,
healing the sick and assuaging passions;
you gave sight to the blind, and raised up
the paralysed man by your divine word,
commanding him at once to walk,
and to take up on his shoulders
the mat he carried. So with him
we all praise you and cry out,
Glory, merciful Christ, to your power!

Strength of body followed
on your commandment, O Christ,
and the man once paralysed was seen
walking briskly and carrying the mat
on which he had lain many years,
praising your great power.

FROM LAUDS

Lord, it was not the pool which healed
the paralysed man, but your word
which made him new; nor did his sickness
of many years oppress him, for the working
of your voice proved more powerful.
He threw away the weight so hard to bear,
and shouldered the burden of his bed,

as testimony to your many mercies.
Glory to you!

The troparion 'Once an angel' from the Canon provides the reason for the choice of this gospel reading during Eastertide. Baptism was at one time celebrated chiefly during the Easter Vigil, and baptismal themes continue into Eastertide. In the story physical healing came from the stirring up of the water of the Sheep Pool; and some of the troparia compare and contrast those waters with the spiritual healing which comes from the water of the font. In baptism Christ gives healing to the soul, that is, to the whole person.

In treating the physical healing of the paralysed man as a sign of the complete healing of the human person, the texts are true to the Gospels. There, and most clearly in St John's Gospel, the miraculous healings attributed to Jesus are signs, pointing to the full healing of the whole person in the kingdom of God. The Bible does not divide human beings into bodies and souls, or bodies, souls and spirits: we are wholes, to be regarded as bodies, souls and spirits, depending on the point of view from which we are seen. It is the whole person who is in need of being made whole; and wholeness, healing and holiness come as we grow in communion with God, with one another and with the whole of creation. God in Jesus Christ enters entirely into his creation, in order to draw it fully into himself. We share in that healing as we grow in communion with Christ through the Holy Spirit, who comes to live in us at baptism. The Spirit's healing power is extended in us as we learn to walk in God's ways, living in accordance with the commandments of love.

6 Mid-Pentecost

Wednesday in the fourth week after Easter

Today is halfway between Easter Day and Pentecost Sunday. The gospel at the Liturgy today is John 7.14–30. This tells of Jesus' appearance at the Feast of Tabernacles, or Booths, an autumn harvest festival lasting seven days (see Leviticus 23.33–36 and Deuteronomy 16.13–15). John says that 'about the middle of the festival Jesus went up into the temple and began to teach'. Despite its occurrence later in the Jewish liturgical year, this episode came to be the principal theme of today's celebration, midway between the Christian versions of the two earlier Jewish feasts, Passover and Pentecost, or the Feast of Weeks.

At the Feast of Booths Jesus stands forth as the Messiah, in whom some believe while others doubt. On the last and great day of the Feast, John says that Jesus cried out, 'Let anyone who is thirsty come to me, and let the one who believes in me drink. As the scripture has said, "Out of the believer's heart shall flow rivers of living water".' John comments, 'Now this he said about the Spirit, which believers in him were to receive.' The theme of thirst and water to satisfy it has already been heard in today's services in verses from the Prophecy of Isaiah read at Vespers, which include 55.1, 'Ho, everyone who thirsts, come to the waters; and you that have no money, come, buy and eat! Come, buy wine and milk without money and without price.' These passages are referred in the Church's tradition to baptism, when the Holy Spirit comes to dwell in those who believe, to satisfy their spiritual thirst and give them salvation. So today's observance is fully in keeping with the baptismal character of Eastertide, although the texts do not make explicit reference to baptism.

FROM VESPERS

We are halfway through the time
which began with the saving resurrection
and will be sealed by Pentecost.
It shines with the brightness of both,
holding both together.
This midpoint we celebrate,
for it displays the coming glory
of the Lord's ascension.

Sion heard and was glad
when Christ's resurrection was proclaimed.
Her faithful children rejoiced
when they saw him wash off
by the power of the Spirit
the stain of Christ's killing.
She makes herself ready,
celebrating the midpoint
between both festivals.

Midway between the feasts
of your resurrection, O Christ,
and of the coming of the Holy Spirit,
we have come together to praise
the mysteries of your miracles.
At this feast send us
your great mercy.

The midpoint has come
of the days of Pentecost,
when Christ, obscurely disclosing
his divine power,
healed the paralysed man by his word
and raised him from his pallet.
As God only can,
he performed a miracle

in a body of clay,
and gave to mortals eternal life
and great mercy.

The Wisdom of God came to the Temple
in the middle of the festival,
teaching and refuting the disobedient Jews,
the Pharisees and the scribes,
and crying out boldly,
Let anyone who is thirsty come to me
and drink living water,
and they will never be thirsty again.
Rivers of eternal life will flow
from the heart of those
who believe in my goodness.
How great are your goodness and mercy,
O Christ our God! Glory to you!

At the midpoint of the feast,
when you, Saviour, were teaching,
the Jews said, How does this man
have such learning,
when he has never been taught?
For they did not know
that you are the wisdom
who created the universe.
Glory to you!

At the midpoint of the feast,
give my thirsty soul to drink
of the waters of reverence;
for you have cried out to all,
Let anyone who is thirsty
come to me and drink.
Glory to you, Christ our God,
Source of life!

FROM MATINS

Halfway through the festival
prescribed by the Law,
you, Christ our God,
the Creator and Lord of all,
said to those who were there,
Come and draw the water of immortality!
So we fall prostrate before you
and in faith we cry out,
Grant us your mercy,
for you are our life's source.

Water my soul, lying fallow
in sins' lawlessness,
with the streams of your blood
and make it bring forth
the fruit of good deeds.
For you, most holy Word of God,
have told everyone to come to you,
and draw the living water of incorruption,
which washes away the sins of those who praise
your glorious and divine resurrection;
for in your goodness you give
to those who know you as God
the power of the Spirit,
who in truth came down from above
on your disciples,
for you are our life's source.

FROM LAUDS

Wisdom and power, reflection of the Father,
eternal Word and Son of God,
you came into the Temple in the flesh
and taught the Jewish people,
strange and hard-hearted.

They were amazed at the wealth
of your wisdom, and cried out,
How does this man have such learning,
when he has never been taught by anyone?

The Lord Messiah silenced the scribes,
refuted the Jews, crying out to them,
You that break the Law,
do not judge by appearances,
like the unrighteous.
For I raised up the paralysed man
on the Sabbath, because I am Lord
of the Sabbath and of the Law.
Why do you seek to kill me,
who raised the dead?

The ungrateful assembly of the Jews,
strange and lawless, stoned Moses,
cut Isaiah in two with a wooden sword,
threw wise Jeremiah into the mud.
They raised the Lord on the cross
and cried out,
You who would destroy the Temple,
save yourself, and we will believe in you.

Brothers and sisters, enlightened
by the resurrection of Christ our Saviour,
we have reached the midpoint
of the Lord's festival.
Let us truly keep God's commandments,
so that we may fitly celebrate his ascension,
and arrive in due course
at the descent of the Holy Spirit.

The texts for the midpoint of the Fifty Days of Easter –
Pentecost in its primary sense – appropriately bring together
the major themes celebrated during Eastertide. The liturgical

calendar, reflecting St Luke's Gospel, distinguishes resurrection, ascension, and the coming of the Spirit – Pentecost in
its usual sense. But these are only facets of the one salvation
effected by Jesus Christ on the cross, and St John's Gospel
binds them inseparably together. For John, the Spirit is given
on the evening of Easter Day; and, while Mary Magdalen is
told not to touch the Saviour when he meets her in the
garden, since he is not yet ascended, a week later Thomas is
invited to touch Christ's wounded body. For John, it is
Christ's death which is his glorification. That glory is
revealed by the resurrection, which is also his ascension, his
return in glory to the Father. The gift of the Spirit is
consequent upon his glorification on the cross. Today's
services draw together the themes the calendar spreads over
fifty days; and by their references to the healing waters of
Bethesda, and the life-giving waters of the Spirit, they invite
all who celebrate the feast to receive afresh the gift of eternal
life, given in the waters of baptism. Buried with Christ in
baptism, we receive the Spirit who works to raise us from the
death of sin to new and eternal life in Christ, and so to
communion with the Father, the source of healing and life.

7 SUNDAY OF THE SAMARITAN WOMAN

Fifth Sunday after Easter

This Sunday takes its name from the gospel read at the Liturgy, John 4.5–42. It is the first of the long discourses of Jesus in St John's Gospel, and its theme is the living water of eternal life, whose source is Jesus himself. In Christian tradition this passage has been understood as referring to baptism, and to the gift of the Holy Spirit to those washed in the waters of the font. In the Roman rite this gospel passage is read on the third Sunday of Lent in Year A, again because of its traditional association with baptism.

As well as the theme of the Samaritan woman, the texts for today include those of the resurrection of Christ, the Mother of God, and Mid-Pentecost. Canons on all four themes are used at Matins.

In the icon of the day, the woman of Samaria is shown sitting on the well-head. In one hand she holds a pitcher for drawing water, and stretches out the other towards Christ. In front of her is a water jar. Christ is seated on a rock nearby, and blesses the woman. The apostles stand astonished behind him.

FROM VESPERS

> The Source of wonders himself
> came to the well at the sixth hour,
> to give life to Eve's offspring.
> For at the very same hour
> Eve departed from Paradise,
> tricked by the serpent.
> So the Samaritan woman
> came to draw water.

The Saviour saw her and said,
Give me water to drink,
and I will satisfy you
with living water.
She understanding ran to the city,
and at once told the crowds,
Come and see Christ the Lord,
the Saviour of our souls.

When the Lord came to the well
the Samaritan woman asked him
in his compassion,
Give me the water of faith
and I will receive baptism's waters,
joy and redemption.
Glory to you, Life-giving Lord!

The Son and Word of the Father,
who with him has no beginning
and with him is eternal,
the Source of salvation,
came to the well.
A woman of Samaria came to draw water.
When the Saviour saw her he said,
Give me water to drink,
and go, call your husband.
Speaking as though to a human being
and not to God, she tried to conceal herself,
and said, I have no husband.
The Teacher said to her,
You are right in saying,
I have no husband;
for you have had five husbands,
and the one you have now
is not your husband.
She marvelled at this saying,

and ran to the city;
she cried out to the crowds and said,
Come and see the Christ,
who gives to the world great mercy.

By Jacob's well Jesus found
the Samaritan woman, and he
who covers the earth with clouds
asked of her water. O marvel!
He who is borne by the cherubim
spoke with a harlot;
he asked for water, who suspended
the earth above the waters;
he looked for water, he the source
of water's springs and pools.
For he wished to draw to himself
the woman ensnared by the fierce enemy,
and give her the water of life to drink,
who was aflame with improper desires:
for he alone is compassionate
and loves humankind.

Today heaven and earth
are radiant and rejoice;
for Christ has been revealed,
becoming incarnate as a human being,
so that he might rescue Adam
from the curse with all humankind.
Having come to Samaria,
he is regarded with wonder
because of his miracles.
For he who clothes the clouds
with water came to a woman
and asked her for water.
So all we who believe worship him,
who for our sake,

by his own compassionate will,
became poor.

When you appeared on earth,
Christ our God,
in your plan for our salvation
which no words can describe,
the Samaritan woman heard your word,
the word of one who loves humankind;
she left her water jar at the well
and ran back, telling those in the city,
Come and see a man who knows human hearts.
Can he be the Christ we expect,
who has great mercy?

FROM MATINS

When she came in faith to the well
the Samaritan woman saw you,
the water of wisdom.
She drank of you generously,
and inherited the kingdom
which comes from above.
Her repute is eternal.

Let us listen to John,
as he teaches us concerning the mysteries
which took place in Samaria;
how the Lord spoke to a woman
and asked of her water,
although he himself
gathers the waters together,
and reigns with the Father and the Spirit.
He came to search for his own image,
and his praise is eternal.

You came to Samaria,
my all-powerful Saviour,

and spoke to the woman,
asking water to drink,
though you yourself drew water
for the Jews from the broken rock.
You brought her to faith in you;
and now she enjoys life
eternally in heaven.

FROM LAUDS

Let heaven and earth rejoice today,
for Christ has appeared,
incarnate as a human being,
to rescue Adam from the curse
with all the human race.
He came to Samaria
and made himself known by wonders.
He came to the woman,
and he that surrounds the clouds
with water asked of her water.
So all we who believe
worship him who for our sake,
by his own compassionate will,
became poor.

This is what the Lord said
to the Samaritan woman:
If you knew the gift of God,
and who it is that is saying to you,
Give me water to drink,
you would have asked him,
and he would have given you to drink,
so that you would never be thirsty again.

Source of life's beginning,
Jesus our Saviour,

you came to the well
of the patriarch Jacob
and asked water to drink
of the Samaritan woman.
When she told him that Jews
do not share things in common
with Samaritans, the wise Creator
guided her with soft words
rather to ask for eternal water.
When she received it
she told everyone and said,
Come and see him who knows what is hidden,
and is God come in the flesh
to save humankind.

This Sunday continues to celebrate the gift of eternal life, given to believers by God through the death and resurrection of Jesus. The dominant imagery of the texts inspired by the gospel of the Samaritan woman, like those of Mid-Pentecost, is that of the water of life, symbol of salvation. Water is itself a symbol of the Holy Spirit, who comes to live in believers when they are baptized. It is the Holy Spirit whom the Nicene Creed names 'the Lord, the Giver of Life', and who gives us a share in the new life of the kingdom of God. That kingdom is embodied in the risen Jesus, whom the texts praise as the source of eternal life.

He is such because he is one in being with the Father, 'who gives life to all things' and 'alone has immortality' (1 Timothy 6.13, 16). In language which echoes the parable of the lost sheep, the troparion 'Let us listen to John' says that Jesus, the Word of God incarnate, 'came to search for his own image': that is, he who was 'the image of the invisible God' (Colossians 1.15) came to find humankind, Adam, created in the image and likeness of God. Having found him, and united human nature to himself, he renewed it by his death and resurrection. That renewed humanity he now shares with us by the gift of the Holy Spirit.

Today's texts invite our meditation on our own baptism, and on the rich symbolism of water in the Scriptures and in Christian tradition. They remind us of the mystery of the incarnation, by which the Second Person of the Trinity, who is fully God, shares no less fully in our humanity, in order to heal it. That healing, effected once for all on the cross, is applied to all who are willing to receive it by the Holy Spirit, the Third Person of the Trinity. The Spirit, like water, cleanses us from sin; the Spirit, like water, revives us; the Spirit, like water, is poured into us, to fill us with the life of God himself, and make us true daughters and sons of our Creator.

8 SUNDAY OF THE MAN BORN BLIND

Sixth Sunday after Easter

Today's gospel, John 9.1–38, tells the story of the healing of the man born blind. It is the fifth of the signs which Jesus performs in St John's Gospel, and points beyond itself to Jesus as the source of spiritual illumination and insight. In the Roman rite this passage is read on the fourth Sunday of Lent in Year A. In the Orthodox lectionary it continues the baptismal theme of Eastertide, since one of the meanings of baptism is enlightenment. In the patristic period the newly baptized are often called 'those who have been illuminated'. Some of the hymns for today elaborate this theme, while others continue the theme of resurrection, running throughout Eastertide.

The icon of the feast depicts a blind man leaning on a stick outside the walls of Jerusalem. Christ stands before him. He puts one hand on the man's head, and with the other anoints his eyes with the clay made from spittle. The apostles standing behind Christ look on. The blind man is depicted again by a pool, washing his eyes with water.

FROM VESPERS

The man born blind said within himself,
Was I born blind because of my parents' sins?
Or was I born to reveal God's works
because of the Gentiles' lack of faith?
I am incapable of asking whether it is night or day.
My feet have had enough of being stubbed on stones.
For I have not seen the sun shining brightly,
nor the one who created me in his image.
But I entreat you, Christ our God,
Look upon me and have mercy on me.

As he left the Temple,
Jesus found a man blind from birth.
He took pity on him and put mud on his eyes,
and said to him, Go, wash in the pool of Siloam.
He washed, and was able to see,
and gave glory to God.
Those who were close to him asked him,
Who opened your eyes,
which no one with sight has been able to cure?
He cried out and said,
A man called Jesus, he said to me,
Wash in the pool of Siloam,
and I was able to see.
He is in truth Christ, the Messiah,
he of whom Moses spoke in the Law.
He is the Saviour of our souls.

Lord, walking along, you found
a man blind from birth;
and the disciples in amazement
asked you, saying:
Who sinned, this man, or his parents,
that he was born blind?
But you, my Saviour, said to them,
Neither this man nor his parents sinned,
but so that God's works might be revealed in him.
I must do the works of him who sent me,
which no one else can do.
When he had said this,
he spat on the ground and made mud,
and spread it on his eyes, telling him,
Go, wash in the pool of Siloam.
He went and washed and was healed,
and cried out to you,
Lord, I believe, and worshipped you.
So we too cry out, Have mercy on us.

Reckoning his whole life night,
the blind man cried out to you, Lord,
Open my eyes, Son of David, our Saviour,
that, with all, I too may praise your power.
Spiritual Sun of righteousness,
Christ our God, by your most holy touch
you gave physical and spiritual sight
to the man deprived of light from birth.
Enlighten us and reveal us as children of the day,
that with faith we may cry out to you,
Great and beyond telling is your compassion towards us:
you love humanity, yours be the glory!

FROM MATINS

The Saviour performed amazing miracles,
and healed the man blind from birth,
spreading mud on his eyes and saying,
Go and wash in the pool of Siloam,
so that you may know me to be God,
going about on earth in human form,
in merciful compassion.

Opening the eyes of him
who could not see the light
perceived by the senses,
you enlightened his spiritual sight,
and caused him to praise you,
recognizing you as the Creator,
in your compassion appearing as human.

Spiritually blind, I come to you,
O Christ, like the man blind from birth,
and in penitence I cry out to you,
You are the brilliant light
of those in darkness.

79

Give me, O Christ,
the stream of wisdom past telling
and of knowledge from on high;
for you are the light of those in darkness
and the guide of those who go astray.
So may I tell those things I have learnt
from the holy book, the gospel of peace,
that is, the miracle of the blind man.
For he was blind from birth,
and received sight both physical and spiritual.
With faith he cried out,
You are the brilliant light
of those in darkness.

Enlighten, Lord,
my spiritual sight,
weakened by dark sin,
mercifully instilling humility,
and cleansing me
with tears of repentance.

Our Saviour, as he went,
found a blind man without sight.
He spat on the ground and made mud,
and spread it on his eyes.
He sent him to Siloam, to go and wash.
He washed and came back,
and saw your light, my Christ.

FROM LAUDS

In your merciful compassion
you became incarnate, Christ our God.
Moved by pity beyond telling,
you bestowed divine radiance
on the man deprived of sight fom birth:

you spread mud on his eyes
with your creative fingers.
Giver of light, enlighten our spiritual senses,
for you alone give with generosity.

Who can tell of your power, O Christ?
Or who can count your many miracles?
For just as in your goodness
you appeared on earth in two natures,
so you gave twofold healing to the sick.
You not only opened the physical eyes
of the man who was blind from birth:
you gave him also spiritual sight.
That was why he testified
that you were God concealed in flesh,
who has mercy in abundance on all.

Our need for salvation includes the healing of our spiritual
blindness. One of the consequences of human sinfulness is
ignorance of God. We live in spiritual darkness, and are
incapable of seeing or knowing God. Jesus Christ brings us
enlightenment. He not only reveals God to us, but enables us
to recognize and acknowledge him. The man born blind is
representative of all humankind. Jesus comes to him, and in
opening his eyes gives him spiritual insight. He recognizes
Jesus as the Christ, the Word of God become flesh, and so
comes to know God, revealed in his incarnate Son.

Illuminating the darkness of sin is no less than an act of
new creation. In the beginning God creates Adam from the
dust of the earth, moistened by mist. Now the incarnate
Word gives sight to the blind by making clay of earth and
spittle. In his love and mercy God our Creator makes himself
known to us, and draws us into a personal relationship with
himself. So our life is renewed, and we become in Christ a
new creation (2 Corinthians 5.17).

Christian tradition associates all the great signs in St John's

Gospel with baptism, for baptism is the sacrament of salvation. The water of the font is the effective symbol of the recreative power of the death and resurrection of Jesus Christ. United with the crucified and risen Christ, Christian believers are healed and made whole, created anew in the image and likeness of their Creator. Like the man born blind, we are enabled through faith to see God in Jesus, and worship him. We pray that God will enlighten our spiritual senses, to perceive him as he comes to us, not only in Christ and in the Church, but in his creation and in our human sisters and brothers.

9 THE ASCENSION

Thursday in the sixth week after Easter

The Ascension is one of the Twelve Great Feasts of the Lord. The Scripture readings at the Liturgy are the accounts of Jesus' ascension into heaven in Acts 1.1–12 and Luke 24.36–53. They provide the main theme of the hymns for the feast, although there are echoes of St John's Gospel, too. Psalm 24 provides the imagery of heaven's gates opening to receive the ascending Christ, to whose victory the reference to Bozrah, from Isaiah 63, in one of the texts from Vespers, makes allusion. That chapter announces God's vindication of his people through bloody conflict. Throughout the texts the one who ascends is understood in terms of the fully developed fifth-century doctrine of the Person of Jesus Christ. He is God the Word who returns to where he has always been, taking with him the human nature he united with himself at his incarnation.

As one of the twelve great feasts, the Ascension is cele-brated for eight days. Throughout this octave it is the chief theme of the daily services. Its celebration comes to an end on the Friday before Pentecost. On that day the texts of the feast itself are sung, from Vespers on Thursday evening to Matins, the Hours and the Liturgy on Friday morning.

The icon of the feast depicts the apostles standing on the Mount of Olives, looking upwards with hands raised in wonder. Although the Acts of the Apostles does not mention her as present, the Mother of God is shown among the apostles, with an angel on either side of her. Clothed in white, they point the apostles to the ascending Christ. Sometimes they hold scrolls, on one of which is written the text, 'Men of Galilee, why do you stand looking up toward heaven?' while on the other is written its continuation, 'This

Jesus, who has been taken up from you into heaven, will come
in the same way as you saw him go into heaven' (Acts 1.11).

FROM VESPERS

The Lord has ascended into heaven,
to send the Paraclete into the world.
The heavens have made ready his throne,
the clouds have prepared his ascent.
Angels are amazed to see a human being
raised higher than themselves.
The Father receives the one
whom he has ever held in his heart.
The Holy Spirit commands all his angels,
Lift up your gates, O rulers!
Clap your hands, all you peoples,
for Christ has ascended where he was before.

Lord, when the apostles saw you, O Christ,
the Giver of life, ascending on the clouds,
they were filled with dejection,
and lamented with tears, saying,
Lord, do not leave us orphans,
for in pity you have loved your servants,
since you are compassionate.
But send us your Holy Spirit,
as you have promised,
to enlighten us.

Most sweet Jesus, you did not leave
the Father's heart, while as a mortal
you lived among mortals.
Today from the Mount of Olives
you were taken up in glory;
in compassion you exalted our fallen nature,
and seated us on God's own throne.

At this the heavenly orders of angels
were amazed, awe-struck at the marvel.
Astonished, they praised your love for humanity.
We on earth join with them
to glorify your descent among us
and your ascension from us,
and we pray: At your ascension
you filled with endless joy your disciples
and the Mother of God who gave you birth:
at their intercession enable us,
in your great mercy,
to share the joy of your chosen ones.

Your angels, Lord, said to the apostles,
Men of Galilee, why do you stand
looking up toward heaven? The one
who has been taken up from you into heaven
is Christ and God;
he will come again in the same way
as you saw him go into heaven.
Worship him in holiness and righteousness.

Adam's nature had fallen
into the lower parts of the earth.
You, O God, have yourself renewed it,
and today you have exalted it
above all rulers and all authorities.
Because you loved us,
you seated us beside you;
because you had mercy on us,
you joined us to yourself;
being one with us,
you suffered with us;
and suffering with us –
although incapable of suffering –
you glorified us with yourself.

But the angels said,
Who is this handsome man?
For it is not a human being only who appears,
but a human being and God, in both natures.
The awe-inspiring angels, then, hovered
in white robes around the disciples
and said, Men of Galilee,
this Jesus, who has gone away from you,
who is both human and God, the God-man,
will come again as judge of living and dead;
he will give to those who have faith
forgiveness of sins and great mercy.

When you ascended, O Christ,
from the Mount of Olives,
the heavenly powers saw you
and cried out one to another,
Who is this? They answered each other,
This is he who is strong and powerful,
he who is mighty in battle,
he who is in truth the King of glory.
But why are his robes red?
He has come from Bozrah,
who is indeed of flesh.
But he himself as God is seated
at the right hand of the Greatness,
and has sent us the Holy Spirit,
to guide us and save us.

FROM MATINS

God before all ages and without beginning,
who took to himself human nature
and mystically deified it,
today ascended. Angels went before
and directed the apostles' gaze towards him

as he went into heaven with great glory.
They worshipped him and said,
Glory to God who has ascended!

You came down to earth from heaven,
and as God you raised up Adam's form,
which lay in Hades' prison;
at your ascension, O Christ,
you exalted that form to heaven,
and placed it on your Father's throne,
for you are merciful and love humanity.

Today the powers above
saw our nature in heaven
and marvelled at this strange ascent.
At a loss, they said one to another,
Who is this who comes?
When they saw their true Lord,
they commanded the gates of heaven
to be lifted up. With these powers
we praise you without ceasing,
for you will come again in flesh,
as judge of all and God almighty.

You fulfilled God's plan for us,
uniting things earthly and heavenly,
and ascended in glory, Christ our God,
to the heavens you never left.
Yet you are not far from us,
for you cry out to those who love you,
I am with you, and no one is against you.

Leaving on earth things earthly,
letting ashes return to their dust,
let us wake out of sleep,
and lift up our sight and our thought.
Let us raise our mortal gaze and senses

to the gates of heaven.
Let us imagine ourselves on the Mount of Olives,
gazing intently at the Redeemer
as he is borne on the cloud.
For thence the Lord went up to heaven;
and there he who loves to give
gave gifts to his apostles;
he spoke to them like a father,
and strengthened them.
He gave them instructions as sons
and said to them, I will not leave you,
I am with you and no one is against you!

FROM LAUDS

Like angels let us celebrate,
we who are of this world,
and sing praise to God,
who sits on his throne of glory:
Holy are you, heavenly Father!
Holy are you, coeternal Word!
Holy are you, Holy Spirit!

The captains of the angels,
perceiving, Saviour, the strange ascension,
said one to another, What sight is this?
In appearance he seems to be human;
but he ascends as though God, with his body,
far above the heavens.

The Galileans saw you, O Word, ascend
from the Mount of Olives with your body,
and heard angels calling to them,
Why do you stand looking?
He will come again in flesh,
just as you saw him go.

You were born as you yourself willed;
you were manifested as you decreed;
you suffered in the flesh, who are our God;
you rose from the dead, destroying death;
you ascended in glory, who fill all things;
and you sent us the divine Spirit,
that we might praise and glorify your Godhead.

The ascension of Jesus has a twofold significance. It is first of all the return to the Father of the Word of God, who, as St John says in the Prologue to his Gospel, 'was with God and [...] was God'. For us and for our salvation he came down from heaven, and 'became flesh and lived among us'. By way of the cross and resurrection, the incarnate divine Son returns to the Father, whose side as God he had never left. The passage beginning 'You fulfilled God's plan for us' gives clear expression to this paradox of the incarnation in traditional Christian thought.

Yet the Son did not return to the Father as he was when he came. He took back to heaven the human nature he had taken to himself in his incarnation. That humanity is now inseparable from him. In Orthodox theology and spirituality the ascension is as much about the exaltation of humanity as it is about the return of the victorious Word to his Father. The nineteenth-century Anglican bishop, Christopher Wordsworth, gave fine expression to that faith in a hymn which includes this verse:

Thou hast raised our human nature
In the clouds to God's right hand;
There we sit in heavenly places,
There with thee in glory stand;
Jesus reigns, adored by angels;
Man with God is on the throne;
Mighty Lord, in thine ascension
We by faith behold our own.

The Ascension celebrates the dignity of human nature, created and created anew by God. Yet that dignity has still to be achieved in individual human beings. The Letter to the Colossians puts it thus:

> So if you have been raised with Christ, seek the things that are above, where Christ is, seated at the right hand of God. Set your minds on things that are above, not on things that are on earth. For you have died, and your life is hidden with Christ in God. When Christ who is your life is revealed, then you also will be revealed with him in glory. (Colossians 3.1–4)

It is the work of the Holy Spirit, living within us since our baptism, to renew our own individual humanity, and conform it more and more to the glorious humanity of Jesus Christ. When all things are gathered up in Christ (Ephesians 1.10), our own humanity will be perfected in his.

10 Sunday of the Three hundred and eighteen fathers of the Council of Nicaea

This Sunday, like all the Sundays in Eastertide, continues to celebrate the resurrection of Jesus Christ, together with his ascension. In addition, it commemorates the Council of Nicaea of 325, the first Ecumenical Synod, or Council. The Council was called to resolve the theological controversy stirred up by the teaching of the Alexandrian presbyter Arius and his followers. Arius explicitly subordinated the Son to the Father. Led principally by Athanasius, deacon and then Bishop of Alexandria, his opponents upheld the equality of the Son with the Father, and defined the Son as 'of one substance' or 'one in being' (*homoousios* in Greek) with the Father, who begets him from all eternity. The hymns which celebrate the Council's victory over Arius and his teaching embody the Council's doctrine, and reflect the Church's mature doctrine of God as Trinity. That teaching was fully established at the Second Ecumenical Council of Constantinople in 381, which proclaimed the Holy Spirit consubstantial with the Father and the Son.

The first reading at the Liturgy, Acts 20.16–18, 28–37, includes Paul's warning to the church at Ephesus to beware of the savage wolves who will come among them, not sparing the flock. The gospel is John 17.1–14, in which Jesus says he has guarded all whom the Father had given him, 'and not one of them was lost except the one destined to be lost'. The original reference is to Judas. Both passages are applied to Arius, who in the Church's tradition became the arch-heretic and betrayer of Christ.

All the ecumenical councils came to feature in Orthodox iconography. In the icon of the Council of Nicaea the Emperor Constantine is depicted enthroned, the bishops seated around him. Among them are Silvester of Rome and Alexander of Alexandria. In the midst is a philosopher, who stands astonished before St Spyridon. In one hand he holds a brick from which come fire and water. The fire goes upward, the water runs down between his fingers. Arius is in front, and before him St Nicholas stands, hand raised to strike him down. The followers of Arius are seated below St Athanasius, shown as a beardless young man. He sits writing the Nicene Creed, from 'I believe in one God' up to 'and in the Holy Spirit'.

FROM VESPERS

When you ascended the cross,
you won victory over hell;
so that, free among the dead,
you might raise up with yourself
those who sat in death's darkness.
Almighty Saviour, you draw life
from the well of your own light:
have mercy on us!

Where can we sinners flee from you, Lord,
for you are present in all creation?
To heaven? That is your home.
To hell? You have defeated Death.
To the depths of the sea? Your hand, Lord, is there.
We come to you for refuge,
and prostrate before you we pray:
You have risen from the dead,
have mercy on us!

The Lord has ascended to heaven,
to send the Advocate to the world.
The heavens prepared his throne,
the clouds his ascension.

The angels are amazed,
for they see a man exalted above themselves.
The Father welcomes the One
whom he holds in his heart eternally.
The Holy Spirit commands all his angels,
Lift up your gates, O rulers!
All peoples, clap your hands!
For Christ has gone up
to where he was before.

From the womb were you begotten
before the morning star,
without mother from the Father
before the world began:
even if Arius thought you created, not God,
and dared in his folly to rank you,
the Creator, among created beings.
So he stored up for himself
the fire that burns for ever.
But the Council of Nicaea, Lord,
proclaimed you Son of God,
sharing the Father's and the Spirit's throne.

Who tore your tunic, Saviour?
Arius, you said, who divided
the Trinity's sovereignty, honoured as one.
He denied you were One of the Trinity;
he taught Nestorius to refuse
to call Mary Mother of God.
But the Council of Nicaea, Lord,
proclaimed you Son of God,
sharing the Father's and the Spirit's throne.

Crazed Arius divided the single sovereignty
of the Most Holy Trinity into three beings,
unlike each other and of different kind.

The Fathers inspired by God came quickly together,
like Elijah the Tishbite burning with zeal;
with the sword of the Spirit they cut through the
    teaching
of the one who taught the shameful blasphemy,
in accordance with what the Spirit plainly declared.

Who will not call you blessed, most holy Virgin?
who will not praise your most pure giving birth?
For the only-begotten Son,
who shone forth from the Father,
has come forth from you, O Pure One,
and become human in a way beyond telling.
By nature he is God, and through nature
has he become human for our sake.
He is not divided into two persons,
but is known without confusion in two persons.
O Pure One most blessed,
pray to him to have mercy on us.

When Christ willed to raise us
from our fallen state of old,
he was nailed to a cross
and laid in a tomb.
The women bringing spices
came tearfully looking for him
and lamenting him said,
Alas, Saviour of all!
How could you accept to lie in a grave?
Once you had willed to lie there,
how could you be taken away?
How could you be moved?
What place conceals your life-giving body?
But Lord, as you promised,
reveal yourself to us
and dry our mournful tears.

While they lamented an angel cried out to them,
Stop your lamenting and tell the apostles,
the Lord has arisen and given to the world
reconciliation and abundant mercy.

Let us, the assembled body of the Orthodox,
celebrate with reverence and in faith
today's yearly commemoration
of the Fathers inspired by God,
who gathered from all over the world
in the glorious city of Nicaea.
For by their reverent thought
they destroyed wicked Arius' godless doctrine,
and in synod expelled him from the Catholic Church.
They taught everyone clearly to acknowledge
that from all eternity the Son of God
is of one being and co-eternal with the Father.
They clearly and reverently set out this teaching
in the Creed, the Symbol of the faith.
So we, following their inspired teaching,
stand firm in the faith, and with the Father
worship the Son and the Holy Spirit,
consubstantial Trinity in one Deity.

Lord, when in your goodness you had fulfilled
the mystery hidden from all eternity and from the
Gentiles,
you came with your disciples to the Mount of Olives,
together with her who gave you birth,
you, the maker and creator of all things.
For it was right that she who as a mother
suffered most because of your passion
should, when your body was glorified,
rejoice with the greatest joy.
We too share that joy, Lord,
because of your ascension into heaven,

and we glorify your great mercy
which has been shown to us.

FROM MATINS

Lord, outside your tomb
Mary Magdalen stood and wept.
Believing you to be the gardener she cried out,
Where have you laid Life Eternal?
Where have you hidden him
who sits on the cherubim throne?
For those who guarded him
have become like dead men for fear.
Either give me my Lord,
or else cry out with me,
You were among the dead
and you have raised up the dead:
Glory to you!

The Apostles' proclamation and the Fathers' teaching
have strengthened the Church's single faith.
Clad in the garment of truth, woven
from knowledge of God from on high,
she handles aright and glorifies
the great mystery of our religion.

Let us listen to the Church of God
as she makes exalted proclamation:
Let anyone who is thirsty come to me and drink.
The cup I hold is the cup of wisdom;
its drink have I mixed with the word of truth,
pouring forth the water
not of contention but of confession.
Drinking of it the Israel which now is
beholds God saying, See, see
that it is I myself and I change not.

I am God, the first and the last,
and besides me there is no other at all.
Those who partake of this shall be satisfied,
and shall praise the great mystery of our religion.

Long ago on the sea of Tiberias,
the sons of Zebedee, Nathanael, Peter,
with two other disciples and Thomas
went fishing. At Jesus' command
they cast the net to the right side
and caught a great quantity of fish.
When Peter recognized him,
he jumped into the sea to go to him.
Appearing to them for the third time,
Jesus showed them bread,
and fish on a charcoal fire.

Today we commemorate the holy fathers,
and ask you, Lord, in your great mercy
at their intercession to deliver your people
from the harm of every heresy;
and count us all worthy to praise
the Father, the Word and the Holy Spirit.

While the disciples looked on
you ascended, O Christ, to the Father,
sitting together with him.
The angels went before you and cried out,
Lift up the gates, lift them up!
For the King has gone up
to the glory, the source of light.

AT LAUDS

The company of the holy fathers,
gathered together from the ends of the earth,
decreed the one being and nature

of Father, Son and Holy Spirit,
and gave clearly to the Church
the mystery of the knowledge of God.
With faith we praise them
and call them blessed, as we say,
O warriors in the Lord's army,
drawn up in divine ranks,
speaking of God;
shining stars of the spiritual firmament;
impregnable towers of the mystical Sion;
sweet-scented flowers of Paradise;
golden mouths of the Word;
boast of Nicaea, the world's adornment,
pray fervently for our souls.

The New Testament witnesses to Jesus as the Son of God, who died, was raised from the dead, and ascended into heaven. By his death and resurrection, and by the coming of the Holy Spirit, he has reconciled all who believe in him, and potentially all humankind, to the Father. That is the faith which inspired all the writings of the New Testament.

But who precisely was Jesus? Humanly speaking, he was a descendant of David, 'born of woman', as Paul says (Galatians 4.4). Christians believed him to be the Messiah, the one sent by God to redeem Israel from slavery to sin. By raising him from the dead, God made the crucified Jesus both Lord and Messiah (Acts 2.36). But that still left his precise relationship with God, with the Father, uncertain. The writers of the New Testament, for the most part Jews, believed firmly that God was one. Yet Jesus had a relationship with God unlike that of any other human being. John depicts a relationship so close that in his Gospel Jesus can say 'the Father is in me and I am in the Father' (10.38) and 'The Father and I are one' (10.30). On the other hand, John can also have Jesus say 'If you loved me, you would rejoice that I am going to the Father, because the Father is greater than I' (14.28).

From earliest times Jesus was worshipped, and Christians prayed to him. That implied he was on a level with God. But in the first three centuries there was an implicit subordination of the Son, and of the Holy Spirit, to the Father. It required Arius' explicit affirmation that the Son was a creature, albeit the highest of all God's creatures, to compel the Church to express with absolute clarity the belief already expessed by Paul, that 'in Christ God was reconciling the world to himself' (2 Corinthians 5.19). Biblical terminology was insufficient – Arius could quote texts such as John 14.28 cited above. The Council of Nicaea adopted the term *homoousios* to express and defend the Church's faith that in Jesus Christ God himself came into the world to save the world. Jesus Christ is 'of one being' with the Father; and the Holy Spirit too is 'of one being' with both the Father and the Son. 'Glory be to the Father and to the Son and to the Holy Spirit' gave liturgical and prayerful expression to the faith of the Church in God as Trinity, as Three Persons and yet one God.

That faith had always been implicit in the Church's liturgical worship and in Christian personal prayer. The doctrine defined and accepted by the 318 holy fathers of Nicaea made that faith explicit. In the Orthodox tradition the teaching of Nicaea is celebrated liturgically, not only in the texts for this Sunday, but in hymns used throughout the liturgical year. It is an intellectual affirmation which safeguards the reality of salvation. That reality is summed up in a sentence attributed to Athanasius of Alexandria, and widely used after him: 'God became human, so that humanity might become divine.' In the Orthodox tradition salvation is understood as deification: the destiny of human persons is to share in the life of God himself. United by the Holy Spirit with the risen and ascended Christ, we share with him in the life of the Father. This is the great mystery of the Christian religion.

11 SUNDAY OF PENTECOST

Pentecost Sunday is the fiftieth day after Easter. At the Liturgy the epistle is Acts 2.1–12. In Luke's account, the disciples 'were all together in one place'. A sound 'like the rush of a mighty wind [...] filled the entire house where they were sitting. Divided tongues, as of fire, appeared among them, and a tongue rested on each of them. All of them were filled with the Holy Spirit and began to speak in other languages [...] about God's deeds of power.' Some of the hymns for today take their theme from this passage. The gospel is John 7.37–52, with 8.12. Jesus proclaims himself the source of the living water, which is the Spirit, to be given to those who believe in him. In the last verse of the gospel, Jesus proclaims himself the light of the world. The light of the Spirit, source of life, is another theme taken up by many of the hymns for today.

Prominent in today's services is the praise of God, whose self-revelation as Father, Son and Holy Spirit is completed at Pentecost. In the Orthodox tradition, Pentecost Sunday is the celebration, not only of the Holy Spirit, but of God as Three Persons; and many of the hymns echo the language of fourth-century trinitarian theology. In popular Russian Orthodox parlance – though not in the service books – today is often called Trinity Day, and Monday is regarded as the specific celebration of the Holy Spirit. Vespers of Monday is usually celebrated immediately after the Sunday Liturgy, rather than in the evening. It is popularly known as the kneeling service, since all kneel while seven long prayers of intercession are recited. They ask for forgiveness, and grace to live in obedience to the commandments and in the hope of resurrection to eternal life; and include prayer for the departed, and those imprisoned in hell.

Churches and homes are traditionally decorated with green branches and flowers on Pentecost Sunday. They symbolize the new life which comes to humankind through the indwelling of the Holy Spirit. The icon of the feast depicts a house in which the twelve apostles are sitting in a semi-circle around the empty throne of Christ. Above the house the Holy Spirit is depicted as a dove, from which twelve tongues of flame come down to rest on each of the apostles. Beneath them is a dark chamber, in which sits an old man, wearing a crown, and holding twelve scrolls on a veil between his hands. He symbolizes the cosmos, the world, in a state of captivity, and stretches out his hands to the light above. That light is the gospel of salvation proclaimed by the twelve apostles, represented by the twelve scrolls.

FROM VESPERS

The Holy Spirit provides all things.
He is prophecies' source
and priests' hallowing.
The unlettered he teaches wisdom,
fishermen he makes theologians.
He holds together the whole order of the church.
One in being and majesty
with the Father and the Son,
Holy Spirit, glory to you!

We have seen the true light,
we have received the heavenly Spirit,
we have found the true faith,
as we worship the undivided Trinity.
For the same has saved us.

In your courts, O Lord,
we who believe in you
bow before you in soul and body;

and we praise you,
the Father without beginning,
the Son also without beginning,
and the co-eternal Holy Spirit,
who illumines and sanctifies us.

Come, you peoples, let us worship
the Godhead in three persons,
the Son in the Father with the Holy Spirit.
For the Father eternally begets the Son,
co-eternal with him and with him enthroned;
and the Holy Spirit is in the Father,
glorified together with the Son:
one power, one being, one Godhead,
whom we all worship, saying, Holy is God,
who has created all things through the Son,
with the co-operation of the Holy Spirit;
Holy is the Mighty One,
through whom we have known the Father,
and the Holy Spirit has come into the world;
Holy is the Immortal One, the Holy Spirit the
    Advocate,
who proceeds from the Father and rests on the Son.
Holy Trinity, glory to you!

When you sent your Spirit, Lord,
on the waiting apostles, the children
of the Hebrews saw it and were terrified,
for they heard them speak in other languages,
as the Spirit gave them ability.
For although they had no education,
they were given understanding.
They captured the pagans for the faith,
and spoke openly of the things of God.
So we too cry out to you,
You have appeared on earth

and saved us from deceit:
glory to you, Lord!

Heavenly King, Advocate, Spirit of Truth,
you are everywhere and fill all things,
the treasure-store of all good things,
and giver of life.
Come and make your home in us,
cleanse us from every stain of sin,
and in your goodness save us.

Languages were once confused,
for the audacious tower's building.
Languages now are understood,
through the glorious knowledge of God.
There God punished the ungodly for their error;
here Christ enlightens the fishermen with the Spirit.
Then lack of speech worked to punish;
now harmony of sound is restored,
for our salvation.

FROM MATINS

Radiant with joy let us who believe
celebrate the feast which completes
all those it comes after: Pentecost,
promise and appointed time's fulfilling.
For at this time the Advocate's fire came
suddenly down to earth as it were in tongues;
it enlightened the disciples and gave them
knowledge of heavenly mysteries.
The Advocate's light came
and enlightened the world.

Lord of lords, one alone from the only one,
Word who came forth from the Father,
the cause of all, himself uncaused,

you always show kindness, so you sent
your undoubted Spirit, equal in power, to the apostles
as they sing, Glory to your power, O Lord.

The divine water of rebirth you mingled
by a word with my created nature,
and poured out for me the stream
from your most pure side, O Word of God,
and sealed me with the warmth of the Spirit.

All things bow the knee to the Advocate,
the Father's offspring, one with the Father in nature.
For in three persons have they assuredly known
the one Being, eternal, unapproachable.
For the grace of the Spirit has caused light to shine.

Worship the supreme Deity, all you who serve
the Being resplendent with threefold light.
For Christ as benefactor works marvellously
and radiant with fire for salvation
supplies the whole grace of the Spirit.

When the Most High came down
and confused the languages,
he scattered abroad the nations.
When he divided the tongues of fire,
he called us all into unity,
and with one voice we glorify the Holy Spirit.

Give speedy and steady consolation, O Jesus,
to your servants when our spirits are sad.
Do not abandon us in affliction,
nor be far from our thoughts
when we are in difficulties,
but always be with us in need.
You are everywhere: draw near to us, draw near;
as you were always with your disciples,

so in your mercy join yourself to us
who desire you; so that, united with you,
we may praise and glorify your Holy Spirit.

Most Holy Spirit,
who proceeds from the Father
and through the Son came to dwell
in the unlettered disciples,
save and sanctify, O God,
all who have come to know you.

Light is the Father, light the Word,
light too the Holy Spirit,
who in fiery tongues
was sent to the apostles,
and through whom the whole world
has been enlightened,
to honour the Holy Trinity.

AT LAUDS

Wonderful things have all the peoples
seen today in the city of David,
when the Holy Spirit came down
in fiery tongues, described by Luke,
who spoke of God. For he said,
When Christ's disciples were all together,
there came a sound like the rush of a violent wind,
and it filled the house where they were sitting.
And they all began to speak in strange words,
strange doctrines, strange teachings,
of the Holy Trinity.

The Holy Spirit always was, and is, and will be,
without beginning and without end,
but always united and counted
with the Father and the Son.

Life and creator of life,
Light and shedder of light,
Goodness and source of goodness;
through whom the Father is made known
and the Son is glorifed and known by all,
one power, one single being, one worship
of the Holy Trinity.

The Holy Spirit is light and life,
the living source of mind;
Spirit of wisdom, Spirit of understanding;
good, of right understanding, in command,
who cleanses sins;
himself God and imparting divinity;
fire, from fire proceeding, who speaks,
works and distributes gifts;
through whom were crowned all the prophets,
and God's apostles together with the martyrs;
amazing hearing, amazing seeing,
fire which distributes itself
to bestow gifts of grace.

The coming of the Holy Spirit at Pentecost fulfils not only
the promise of Jesus, but also the promise made by God under
the first covenant. The Jewish celebration of Pentecost came
to commemorate the giving of the Law at Sinai, and the
making of the covenant between God and his people. The
prophets, inspired by the Spirit, looked forward to a renewed
covenant, when God's law would be written, not on tablets of
stone, but on human hearts. Christians understand Pentecost
to be the fulfilment of that hope. The Holy Spirit not only
gives believers insight into the purpose of God, but also
enables them willingly to obey the divine law of love.

The Spirit works to overcome division and unite God's
people in his love. Several of the hymns contrast Pentecost
with the Tower of Babel. There, human sin caused division,

and mutual lack of comprehension. The coming of the Spirit brings forgiveness and reconciliation with God, and so unites people of different languages and cultures in a common understanding of God's mighty works.

Above all, the coming of the Holy Spirit completes God's self-revelation to humankind. God is not simply God, he is Father, Son and Holy Spirit. Christian trinitarian theological terminology can seem remote from the reality of a God whom Christians believe to be love. But that terminology was elaborated in the course of the theological controversies of the fourth century, and in particular at the Council of Nicaea in 325 and the Council of Constantinople in 381, in order to safeguard the Christian experience of God. The Jews believed in a God whom they addressed as Father, and who was passionate in his love for his people. The first disciples, devout Jews, found themselves compelled by their experience of Jesus to believe that in his person they had encountered the Son of God, who was not less than his Father, though clearly distinct from him. In the same way, after his death and resurrection, they experienced in the Holy Spirit the presence both of the Son and the Father. Yet the Spirit was clearly distinct from the Son as well as from the Father. In their experience of Father, Son and Holy Spirit they experienced the same divine love. The love of the Father was embodied in the Son, and he gave his life on the cross to reconcile repentant sinners to the Father. The same love was present in the Holy Spirit, who enables human beings to recognize God in Christ, and to share in the life and love of God himself.

To affirm that God is Trinity is to affirm that God is love, who reaches out to us in love, and lovingly draws us into his own life. That is the essence of Christian faith, and it is expressed visually in the icon of the Trinity painted by Andrei Rublev. The three angels, who visited Abraham at the Oak of Mamre in Genesis 18, are seated on three sides of a table, in form an altar. The sole dish on the table contains the head of a sacrificial calf, eucharistic symbol of the self-giving love which is the heart of God. The fourth side of the table, facing the worshipper, is empty. God calls each of us to occupy it, and to share in the divine life, at whose heart is the love of Father, Son and Holy Spirit for each other and for all creation.

12 SUNDAY OF ALL THE SAINTS

The first Sunday after Pentecost is the commemoration of all the saints. The epistle is Hebrews 11.33—12.2b, the composite gospel is made up of Matthew 10.32–34, 37–39, 19.27–30. The former chronicles many of the heroes of the Old Testament, who form the great cloud of witnesses which surrounds the followers of Jesus, as they run the race set before them. The latter promises the reward of life for those who acknowledge Jesus before their contemporaries, love him before all others, and take up their cross and follow him. They will inherit eternal life in the new world, where the Son of Man is enthroned in glory, and the apostles judge the twelve tribes of Israel.

The icon of the feast depicts a synaxis, or gathering, of holy men and women.

FROM VESPERS

> Orators of the Spirit, the Saviour's disciples
> became by faith the Spirit's instruments;
> scattered abroad to the ends of the earth,
> they sowed the word of orthodox teaching.
> From it, by God's cultivation and grace,
> there grew the ranks of martyrs, imaging
> the venerated passion by many kinds
> of torture, flogging and burning.
> Boldly they intercede for us.
>
> Those who in every place fought in faith,
> apostles, martyrs, priests wise in God's knowledge,
> revered women, the holy gathering,

these let us duly praise with holy songs.
For those on earth have been united
with those in heaven; and by Christ's grace
by their passion they have attained
impassibility. Now like sparkling stars
they give us light, and boldly intercede for us.

Divine army of martyrs,
Church's foundation, gospel's completion,
by your deeds you have fulfilled
the Saviour's words. For through you
have been closed the gates of Hades,
opened against the Church;
your blood poured out has dried up
the idols' libations; your death
has brought many believers to birth.
You have amazed the angels, you stand
crowned in the presence of God.
Intercede continually with him for us.

United in faith let us celebrate the universal festival
of those who from the beginning have pleased God:
the patriarchs held in honour, the prophets' company,
the apostles' crowning glory, the army of martyrs,
the ascetics' boast, the memory of all the saints;
since they intercede constantly for the world's peace
and for abundant mercy to be shown to us.

Let us who believe come eagerly together
for this festival; for a mystical bowl
is set before us, and a spiritual banquet filled
with the good cheer of delectable dishes –
the martyrs' mighty deeds. For, strong in spirit,
from all earth's bounds they offered to God,
regardless of age, the spiritual sacrifice
of limbs subjected to all kinds of torture.

Some had their heads cut off, while others
had their hands and arms torn from their joints,
all the saints becoming partakers of Christ's sufferings.
But, Lord, as you repaid them crowns for tortures,
so deem us fit to follow in their steps,
for you love humankind.

Come, all you faithful, let us keep
today's festival with reverence,
and let us gloriously honour the glorious
and venerable memory of all the saints, saying:
Hail, glorious apostles, prophets, martyrs and bishops!
Hail, company of saints and righteous!
Hail, band of honoured women!
Intercede with Christ for the world,
that the emperor be victorious over the barbarians,
and that abundant mercy be shown to us.

Dressed as though in purple and fine linen
with the blood of the martyrs throughout the world,
your Church cries out to you,
Christ our God, through them.
Send down on your people your compassion,
give peace to your commonwealth,
and to us your great mercy.

FROM MATINS

Praising the hosts of all your saints,
I pray that by their intercession
my soul may be illumined by your light.
For you are unapproachable light,
and you drive away the darkness of ignorance
by the beams of your own brightness, O Christ,
Word of God and giver of Light.

You have been made beautiful, O Saints,
with the beauty that was from the beginning,

and you have appeared as luminaries
who have not gone astray; and so
you have made Christ's Church heaven,
one in one way, another in another,
adorning her in many different ways.

The company of the saints has been united
with you by love, and delights in you
in purity and holiness. With joy they dance
with the angels in the unending dance
around you, O God and Lord,
whose providence watches over all.

Today we see the company of your saints
illuminated by your brightness, O Saviour,
and by the inextinguishable flame of grace.
So we praise without ceasing your divine riches
and the abundance of your good gifts,
for you love humankind.

The saints in Sion found you, Lord,
a precious and chosen stone,
placed in the head of the corner,
an unshakeable foundation
on which, as chosen stones,
they have built themselves.

The ranks of the saints, giving ceaseless praise
to him who rests among the saints,
now enjoy divine delight; they rejoice
and join in the dance, singing,
Blessed are you, God of our ancestors!

Rejoicing in the brightness none can imagine,
and filled with divine joy and delight,
you, O Saints, are called gods,
because you have drawn near to God;

participants in the sparkling light
of the divine energies,
and illumined by the rays
of the glory which none can tell,
you highly exalt Christ for ever.

Tested by fiery ordeals,
not seduced by pleasures,
you rejoice with perfect joy,
assembly of the saints in heaven,
standing glorious before the Lord's
throne of light; for by truth's appearings
the mirrors have been shattered
and the shadow has passed away.

FROM LAUDS

The Lord has made marvellous
the saints in the world;
for they accepted in their flesh
his marks and sufferings,
by which they were adorned,
and clothed themselves openly
with divine beauty.
Let us praise them
as unfading flowers,
as fixed stars of the Church,
as willing sacrifices.

May they be praised with holy songs!
For apostles with prophets,
teachers with the blessed,
all the righteous with the holy martyrs,
women who have fought the good fight,
and lived as hermits with longing for God,
the multitude of the saints,

113

the hosts of the righteous,
are inheritors of the kingdom of heaven
and citizens of Paradise.

May the martyrs be praised!
For they turned earth into heaven
by the radiance of their noble deeds;
they became like Christ in his death;
they walked in the way that heralds immortality;
they purified human passions by the working of grace;
with one mind they fought with courage
throughout the world.

The fifty days of Easter reach their climax in the feast of Pentecost, the descent of the Holy Spirit on the Church. The liturgical calendar continues with the weeks after Pentecost. The following Sunday is not part of Eastertide, but theologically completes the cycle begun eighteen weeks before, with the Week of the Publican and Pharisee, the first of the pre-Lenten weeks. Those who turn to God in penitence and humility, trusting in his gracious forgiveness and loving power to heal, share through baptism in the death of Christ, and are raised with him to new life in the Holy Spirit. The Holy Spirit lives and works in them to transfigure them into the likeness of Christ, the image of perfected humanity. So they become what the gospel calls them to be, holy men and women, reflecting the love of God in lives conformed to the pattern of Christ's self-giving on the cross.

In the saints, God completes his self-revelation as Trinity. We cannot know God as he is in himself. He is transcendent, beyond human imagining and imaging. But he reveals himself in his Son, in the Word of God who is God, and becomes human in Jesus Christ. 'No one knows the Father except the Son, and any one to whom the Son chooses to reveal him,' says Jesus in Matthew's Gospel (11.27). The Son makes the Father known to us. But it is only by the inspiration of the

Holy Spirit that we can recognize Jesus for what he truly is. 'No one', says Paul, 'can say "Jesus is Lord" except by the Holy Spirit' (1 Corinthians 12.3). The Holy Spirit makes the Son known to us. But how is the Holy Spirit made known to us? To that question the Orthodox tradition answers: in the lives of the saints. In the Western Christian tradition, the Sunday after Pentecost is kept as Trinity Sunday. It celebrates the completion of God's revelation of himself as Three Persons with a doctrinal festival. In the Eastern Christian tradition, the Sunday of All Saints celebrates the personal Spirit's continuing self-revelation in human persons.

That is as it should be. For God does not reveal himself to us for the sake of theological knowledge in the academic sense. He makes himself known to us in the process of saving and healing the human race and all creation, in order to draw all that he creates into his own life and love. True theology is personal knowledge of God, and that knowledge is acquired by prayer and obedience to the commandments. In the Eastern Christian tradition, one who prays is a theologian, and a theologian is one who prays. The goal of prayer, and of the Christian life as a whole, is growth in the knowledge of God; and that growth is given by the Holy Spirit. St Seraphim of Sarov said that the goal of the Christian life is the acquisition of the Holy Spirit: the Spirit who reveals Christ to us, who in turn makes known to us the Father. The Christian life is the life of the Trinity in us, drawing us ever deeper into the life of the Trinity, and so making us saints: human persons becoming healed, whole and holy, renewed in the likeness of God, in whose image we are created.

The Society for Promoting Christian Knowledge (SPCK) was founded in 1698. Its mission statement is:

To promote Christian knowledge by

- **Communicating the Christian faith in its rich diversity**
- **Helping people to understand the Christian faith and to develop their personal faith; and**
- **Equipping Christians for mission and ministry**

SPCK Worldwide serves the Church through Christian literature and communication projects in 100 countries, and provides books for those training for ministry in many parts of the developing world. This worldwide service depends upon the generosity of others and all gifts are spent wholly on ministry programmes, without deductions.

SPCK Bookshops support the life of the Christian community by making available a full range of Christian literature and other resources, providing support for those training for ministry, and assisting bookstalls and book agents throughout the UK.

SPCK Publishing produces Christian books and resources, covering a wide range of inspirational, pastoral, practical and academic subjects. Authors are drawn from many different Christian traditions, and publications aim to meet the needs of a wide variety of readers in the UK and throughout the world.

The Society does not necessarily endorse the individual views contained in its publications, but hopes they stimulate readers to think about and further develop their Christian faith.

For information about the Society, visit our website at *www.spck.org.uk*, or write to:
SPCK, Holy Trinity Church, Marylebone Road,
London NW1 4DU, United Kingdom.